"This book bravely goes where no wom [...] While many will be familiar with the cor [...] ships, few authors have illustrated in such a [...] and personal fashion the value of fantasy, passion and the place it has in our lives. This book encourages us to open and explore who we are, using our romantic attractions as a point of departure."

Karen Lia Schlick, ARTIST, TEACHER, WRITER

"This book is first aid for marriages."

Clare Mastromonaco

". . . an autobiographical and genuinely honest, personal revelation."

Rochelle Lynn Holt

"If you are thinking of having an extramarital affair, read this book first."

Anonymous

"Harms invites each of us to encounter our inner life—the creative dimension of our inner life—that voices the essence of our complex individuality and extends into the outer world and decrees the persons with whom we get involved."

James Strecker, THE ECLECTIC CHAIR

"I found comfort in my sorrows and inspiration in my dreams from the messages that I first discovered in Ms. Harms book. Over time I learned to savor the power of her words through my personal experience . . . If you dare to read The Inner Lover, you will evolve, guaranteed."

Carroll Parrott Blue, Professor, SanDiego State University

"For over four years, Valerie Harms has shared her ideas with me on issues of relationships, the inner life and psychology. Her insights and perspectives challenge her readers to view the world and themselves in a new light."

Susan Bauchner, WOMEN'S DIVISION DIRECTOR, JEWISH FEDERATION OF GREATER PHILADELPHIA

"For women in therapy, this book may be a useful tool for focusing on issues or love, sex, and power relations. . . . appropriate for large psychology collections."

Lucy Patrick, FSU, LIB. FOR LIBRARY JOURNAL

"Valerie opens us to the possibility of living relationship to support and feed our individuality and creativity. . . . I often recommend this book to clients who are struggling with relationships."

Jeanne Cervin, CT PSYCHOTHERAPIST

Other books by Valerie Harms

Your Soul at a Crossroads
(Magic Circle Press, 2013)

Dreaming of Animals
(Magic Circle Press, 2005)

*The National Audubon Society Almanac of the Environment/
The Ecology of Everyday Life*
(Grosset/Putnam, 1994)

Frolic's Dance
(Soundprints, A Smithsonian Heritage Book, 1989)

Beezus and Ramona Diary
(William Morrow Publishers, 1986)

Tryin' To Get To You, The Story of Elvis Presley
(Atheneum Publishers, 1979)

Stars In My Sky/Nin, Montessori, Steloff
(Magic Circle Press, 1977)

Unmasking: Ten Women in Metamorphosis
(Swallow Press, 1973)

The Inner Lover

*Using Passion as a
Way to Self-Empowerment*

VALERIE HARMS

THE INNER LOVER
Using Passion as a Way to Self-Empowerment

Cover photo courtesy of Shutterstock.com.

Grateful acknowledgment is made to the following to reprint previously published material: Michael Hannon for "The Muse," which appeared in *Mamoa: A Pacific Journal of International Writing*, Spring/Fall 1989; Threshold Books, RD 4, Box 600, Putney, VT 05346, for "The Naked Sun," by Jelaluddin Rumi, in *This Longing*, translated by Coleman Barks and John Moyne; Red Ozier Press, 157 Center Road, Woodbridge, CT 06525, for "Why Mira Can't Go Back to Her Old House," in *The Poems of Mirabai*, by Robert Bly; Robert Hass for excerpt from "Privilege of Being," © 1989 by Robert Hass from *Human Wishes* by Robert Hass, first published by the Echo Press in 1989; reprinted by permission.

Published by Magic Circle Press

Print ISBN: 9781625361578
Ebook ISBN: 9781625361561

A C. G. JUNG FOUNDATION BOOK

The C. G. Jung Foundation for Analytical Psychology is dedicated to helping men and women to grow in conscious awareness of the psychological realities in themselves and society, find healing and meaning in their lives and greater depth in their relationships, and to live in response to their discovered sense of purpose. It welcomes the public to attend its lectures, seminars, films, symposia, and workshops and offers a wide selection of books for sale through its bookstore. The Foundation also publishes *Quadrant*, a semiannual journal, and books on Analytical Psychology and related subjects. For information about Foundation programs or membership, please write to the C. G. Jung Foundation, 28 East 39th Street, New York, NY 10016.

Contents

Contents

Preface

The meaning of my existence is that life has addressed a question to me. Or, conversely, I myself am a question which is addressed to the world, and I must communicate my answer, for otherwise I am dependent on the world's answer. That is a suprapersonal life task, which I accomplish only by effort and with difficulty.

— C. G. JUNG, *Memories, Dreams, Reflections*

My concept of the Inner Lover began with a psychoanalytic experience I had in my late thirties. Before then I had the conventional view that love needed to be lived out in actual relationship and that if the bond couldn't grow, it was too bad, but one should leave the sorrow behind and go on to the next relationship as quickly as possible. Meanwhile the marriage I did have with my loved one was filled with wretched conflicts that I was at a loss to transmute.

Through the psychoanalytical experience, I learned something about projections and how the energy of love can be transformed. I also learned that a relationship, even if it was primarily inner, is creative and important, hardly to be ranked a zero. I had gone from having a heart of stone, devoid of Eros, feeling that life was barren and I a bare bone, to a middle stage of softening and even transparency, when I could feel tenderness for another again, and finally to a time of being alone, when my heart opened like a lotus flower. I realized then that vitality, love, and passion were in myself, not dependent on others. I attained a state in which my psyche was suffused with Eros. This blending, which I regard as the ultimate Inner Lover experience, made me feel radiant and peaceful, with no need to extract anything from or cling to another. I was simply devoted to love and being.

Over the years I had puzzled over the differences between the way my desired ones appeared in dreams or fantasies and the way they were in outer life. This duality, I discovered, is actually very revealing. I called it the Inner Lover phenomenon. As a result, I examined my past differently and saw how the imprint of relationships—especially with my father and husband—influenced my experiences with passion and intimacy. I approached future loves with much better understanding. If this knowledge could do such wonders for me, I think it can for others too.

Thus, in this book I attempt to show how the Inner Lover works and how to bring about the union of soul and desire, often using my experiences to illustrate how the Inner Lover gets formed and is different from the outer one. While parts of my romances involve pain and loss, I present them not as failures, but as times when my sense of self greatly expanded.

The defeats and rejections became highly instructive. They obliged me to discover the ever-renewable fireball of energy supporting my passion and creativity. It has turned out that the realm of relationship has, more than anything else, forced me into having the will to live out of my essential nature. Since I see my existence as a question to the world, as Jung said in the epigraph, I have written this book to communicate the answer that I have found so far as part of my own struggles with *individuation*, or the attempt to live out of my own ethics and inner imperatives.

A word about the relevance of subjectivity to truth. Subjective reality is made up of personal memories, feelings, thoughts, and fantasies. I treat feelings, thoughts, awarenesses, and hunches as psychological facts. Persons have them and are influenced by them. Whatever constitutes subjective reality is important psychologically and therefore becomes objective fact. (At the end of part four, "The Wedding," I discuss the science of subjectivity in more detail.)

To dwell on personal thoughts and feelings is criticized by some as being self-absorbed and narcissistic "navel-gazing." To me those critics are mistaken because they do not experience the numinosity or the principles of deeper experience. Many people are afraid of the intensity or possible chaos that lies beneath the surface of conventional attitudes, and they condemn others who dare to realize more of themselves. But the fact is that subjective experience is the very thread through the labyrinth to the wisdom at the center. Real life includes both the inner and outer events.

Anaïs Nin once said, "The personal life deeply lived always extends into truths beyond itself."

This philosophy is a basic tenet of this work.

And so I write about the truths that emerge from subjective experience. I hope this book links readers to their wisdom and power by way of their personal passion and fantasies.

PART ONE

Love Is a Life or Death Matter

Introduction to the Inner Lover

This book delves into the travails as well as the fantasies of love. It is about the heartbreak of love and the dance of love, and the connection between the two. It encourages you to sing your song of love without ever giving up. It shows you how love can be the crowning glory of your life.

As an energy, love is elusive. It is fluid as water, invisible as air, hot as fire. Like the elements, it is vital. For without love we die. Too many of us choose a living death because we are afraid of love. The flights of fun and passion elude us.

Pierre Teilhard de Chardin, the biologist and philosopher, stated that if we could harness the energy of love, we could transform the world. The Inner Lover concept is about harnessing the energy of love within ourselves. If the dynamics are grasped, the world will indeed be transformed also. Physics teaches us that energy cannot be killed, it changes form. So it is with love. We need to understand how it transforms us.

One traverses the landscape of the Inner Lover as on a journey. It begins with the pictures we hold in our minds of the person to whom we're strongly attracted. He or she appears in fantasies and dreams, thoughts and images, usually in solitude when the actual person is not present. However, the inner images have a life of their own, which reflect both the outer relationship and the direction of one's deeper Self or soul. These images constitute the Inner Lover. On the way the Inner Lover brings gifts of creativity to one's being, work, relationships, the whole of life.

It may help to visualize ourselves as a tree. The branches are our outer relationships, the roots are the images and fantasies that reach down into the unconscious source, and the trunk is our body that links the two. Keeping an open flow between the underground roots and healthy manifestations on the surface is the goal.

It is essential to see that the fantasies of love have a dual purpose. One is to instruct us about what is going on in a relationship, and the other is to show us what is going on in our soul. We have to break the old habit of always assuming that the other person is the object of our thoughts, wishes, dreams, and desires.

No one is immune to passionate love for other people, but some will go to great lengths to avoid the emotional turmoil. Sooner or later the consequences of love must be faced and endured, if we wish to grow. How we respond to love, then, becomes a very important issue in our life. Our attractions contain projections of our unconscious potentials, compelling us to new dimensions of experience in the world.

As a relationship develops, on the outer level it may be short or long, an affair or a marriage with children, but it is sure to come up against an obstacle. The other person may be married, may not feel the same way, may be inappropriate professionally, or may die. Once we know how to relate to the image of the Inner Lover, we can receive the love despite what happens in the outer relationship.

We need to stop fighting the feelings that desire brings and surrender to them. When we become attentive to our fantasies and dreams, loving and not condemning our deepest wishes, we give them a chance to direct and empower our lives. Whether our attractions are lived out with other people or not, we will surely tussle with ego attitudes toward our intimate feelings. Dreams especially show us how different parts of our psyche may be in conflict. The aim of figures in our dreams is to reconcile these parts. When we have images of union between ourselves and

4

good lovers, our egos are in alignment with the deeper purposes of our psyches. This inner marriage is worth striving for because it brings ~~safety~~ and ~~security~~. *fun*, *laughter*, *excitement*, *adventure, zest, being alive*

We often think that the pains and difficulties of love originate in the outer situation but they have roots in our intimacy with our selves. If we can attune to our inner figures more, the humiliation and separation from others that we are used to experiencing will lose their shamefulness. The wounds of love are real, but para-doxically, if they are thoroughly endured, they become the source of joy and creativity. Our Inner Lovers want us to lead the most meaningful lives possible and fail us only when we try to avoid our feelings or spontaneous images arising from the unconscious.

In approaching Inner Lovers, we have to understand that inner and outer events are interwoven and simultaneous. As we reflect on them, they yield their treasures, bit by bit seeping into our beings. In the next chapter I will examine how the components of this phenomenon work together.

The Roots of Desire

The Dynamics of Attraction

The perspective of depth psychology assumes that every individual has a unique soul (or psyche) with the potential for growth and that the conscious self makes transactions with the unconscious. No quick fixes, palliatives, behavior modification, or even rigid analysis here. Instead we are in the realm of ever-present instincts and fantasies, a territory first staked out by Sigmund Freud and delineated further by C. G. Jung and others. The focus on dreams and images from the unconscious gives this psychology its "depth" orientation.

Many psychological ideas are part of the cultural currency now. We know that when we relate to someone, there are more than just the two of us present. There are one another's parents and possibly other family members who influence our present interaction. We've learned that we *project*, that is, see in another attitudes or qualities that originate in ourselves. (Our mind is like a film projector that throws onto a screen the images that are running through itself.) We have longed for a "soul-mate" and created havoc in our outer relationships by making impossible demands on another. Anyone who's had the experience of being seen as other than they are knows how uncomfortable this can be.

It is a mistake to expect to find a soul-mate in another person. A real person should be loved for who they are and are becoming as life unfolds. The Inner Lover is the true soul-mate whom we seek for unconditional love and support.

That many of us passionately long for a soul-mate—and that this longing endures—shows the tenacity of our soul's yearning for union with an Inner Lover. If we can focus on the marriage of significant male and female figures in our dreams and images, we will be much better off We will make much better outer bonds as well.

Once we come to know the Inner Lover, we won't lose ourselves in someone else or expect them to be perfect. We will be capable of a deeper love, a more conscious devotion. This relaxes and frees any relationship. On the way to union within we will undoubtedly notice that it can be just as difficult for the inner couple to harmonize as it is for outer couples. But we can rely on our images to reveal to us the truth about our capacity for passion and intimacy and where exactly we need polishing.

Attractions, then, arouse the face of a particular Inner Lover. When the attraction becomes intense, we say we are in love as we have in the past, but now we can look more closely at the images of the person in our thoughts, fantasies, and dreams. Discern the Inner Lover in these pictures. The images will seem to be about the very recognizable person, but they depict events that are different from what happens in outer reality. They thus carry messages about ourselves as well as the relationship.

Before examining further how the realm of fantasy works, it is important to answer this question: *Who is the hook catching your projection and why?*

Projection

When we are attracted to someone, we usually say that person is so wonderful because he or she has such and such qualities. Projection begins with our seeing those qualities in another because we have not yet recognized them in ourselves. They exist in us but have been hidden because they are still in our unconscious.

7

When we are attracted to another person, we can ask ourselves: What qualities am I seeing? What are the ones I need to recognize or develop in myself? To bring them into consciousness in this way is called *owning the projection*.

It is a mistake to criticize ourselves for our projections. Some people, if they feel strongly about another, will say, "I must be projecting," as if it is a spot to be gotten rid of as quickly as possible. Instead, we should embrace our projections, knowing that they are leading somewhere—perhaps to a new relationship, definitely to a new level of being in the world.

Projections can hit us hard and last a long time. They will be emotionally arousing as long as we have something to learn from them. When they lose their force, the relationship with the person may continue—perhaps much more smoothly! Projection, then, first happens outside of us, as we become completely absorbed in all the details concerning another person. The more aware we are, the more consciously we will be able to incorporate the qualities that have attracted us. We will realize that projections have a dual nature—to both involve us with another person as well as bring us messages from the unconscious about potentials for our life.

We thus can be grateful for our projections. Even when our emotions heat to the boiling point, it is worth remembering that to endure them to the end is the way to wisdom. Embracing our desire and projections is clearly a necessary part of self-acceptance. Our projections will turn out to be milestones on our individuation paths. For invariably it takes other people to break through the defended heart.

While our psyches contain images of people of our own sex as well as those of the opposite sex, those of the opposite sex (*contrasexual*) are closer to the unconscious. Jung gave the term *anima* to the image of women that men see in dreams and fantasies and *animus* to women's images of men. He pointed out that they were bridges to deeper layers of the unconscious, carriers of our life's meaning. Thus, when we are intensely attracted to a person, we experience not only the person but also the light of wisdom radiating from the unconscious.

When we give importance to the images and messages of our inner figures, we can align ourselves with our soul purpose. When we are in harmony, our dreams will show us in union with our Inner Lover. Such moments of *coniunctio* (an alchemical term that Jung used as well) indicate a balance between the contra-sexual parts. When dreams and images also show marriages or weddings, they are called sacred or divine because of their numinous power for people's lives. This condition spawns many gifts, a subject which will be taken up more fully in part four of the book.

As we progress on our individuation paths, we will have a variety of Inner Lovers. To paraphrase Emma Jung in *Animus and Anima*, our Inner Lovers will vary according to our development and culture. A young female may be attracted first to a handsome, muscular man. As she develops intellectually, she may want a man who accomplishes important deeds. If a woman incorporates this hero within her, she will become more brave, forceful, and playful. If she does not, she is likely to try to manipulate the man to do what she wants, as well as be nagging, helpless, and conventional in her thinking. Her dreams and images will be full of harsh, critical males, issuing commands, and meting out punishments.

Since our patriarchal culture promotes the idea that women are inferior to men, a woman often has to struggle with lack of courage or will to become spiritually and intellectually independent. In order to be free of the inner tyrant or find supportive figures, she must often rebel against her culture and upbringing.

Many women today still project sexual initiative and satisfaction onto a man. Women would be much happier if they were responsible for attaining their own sexual pleasure. But even very astute and sophisticated women have trouble breaking free from tyrannical inner figures. Some women stay with men who are consistently unfaithful or alcoholic rather than face life alone, while others denounce men behind their backs and at the same time support them. When women take responsibility for their projections, they reclaim much-needed power. Otherwise they literally give it away by centering it all in the outside person.

When a man is dependent on a woman, he tends to let her take care of the relationship and do his feeling for him. (In how many

9

couples do we see the woman doing the gift buying for birthdays and holidays and arranging the social engagements?) His inner images are usually of women who are mothers, sisters, teachers, mistress-slaves, goddess-witches, and half-human enticing beauties. When a man ignores his inner images of women, he is likely to blame his outer woman for his moods and be annoyed, jealous, or possessive when she is not behaving as he thinks she should.

In *A Little Book on the Human Shadow* Robert Bly says: "What other qualities or powers does a man project onto a woman? He may project animal sexuality onto her, in which case she may feel wicked and overly animal; he may project spirituality onto her, in which case she may feel unduly elevated; he may give her his power of weakness, or his insanity. Some men project their competence in the world onto a woman. And many men give their witch to a woman, or to several women."[1]

Other common examples of unaware projection are, for instance, when a man tries to unite with an ideal goddess figure by having sex with a woman and ignoring her individuality; or when a man seeks out women artists as lovers rather than exploring his own talent; or when a man sees a woman as being spiritual and weak in the world, while at the same time he is dependent on her counsel and support.

In all these situations the man is suffering from an undeveloped relation to the feminine within him. The feminine often feels too soft, inferior, and irrational for the man to yield to, so he rejects those reflections. Then his images of women become ferocious beasts. When a man has a highly developed relation to the woman inside him, she will appear as a wisdom figure. The following dream shows a man's positive relation to his inner female: *Anne has made a fire in my fireplace, gathered the wood, cut it to fit the fireplace, and is tending the fire, all on her own. She sits by the fire and feeds it. This is the way I always wanted it to be.*

Those who hook our unconscious projections will show up as figures in our dreams in order to reveal what we need to know in relation to how we are behaving in our lives. If these inner figures are ignored, they will persist in appearing in frightening guises until we start making appropriate adjustments. When we do heed inner figures, they appear gentle and helpful. We also feel less conflicted and more energetic as we go about our day. <u>Our outer relationships are much lighter and freer.</u>

Psyche

The word *psyche* is synonymous with soul and refers to the whole person—body, mind, spirit—as well as all one's complex and diverse conscious and unconscious manifestations. I take *ego, consciousness,* and *self* to be similar in meaning. Each of us has an ego as the center of our knowledge; it comprises all that we are conscious or aware of.

The *unconscious* can be said to be all that is not known as well as the accumulated contents of history since the beginning of evolution. In *The Art of Intimacy* Thomas and Patrick Malone write, "The unconscious perpetuates in humans the wisdom of animals and plants: a wisdom that so perfectly manages breathing, heartbeat, and the intricate chemistry of our human bodies as exquisitely as animal and plant ecologies manage to keep their balance—when not interfered with by us. . . . The unconscious takes us back to the natural by putting us in touch with our nature."[2]

The unconscious produces thoughts and ideas that our consciousness depends on. In the form of dreams and images it balances our ego attitudes and has a purpose of its own that it asserts from time to time, as it does in love. The word *Self is* sometimes awkwardly used to suggest the source or intelligence that weaves the direction of our fate and dreams. For Jung it circumnavigated the conscious and unconscious elements and expressed this totality in symbols of wholeness. Images that reconcile ego with this larger Self are experienced as numinous and portentous.

To some people the unconscious seems threatening. They would prefer to be thrilled by monsters in horror movies or drug-induced fantasies than to look at their own images. To some the unconscious is likely to be a cesspool of rotting corpses and demons. But that attitude is based on ignorance. The unconscious threatens destruction when unheeded. When we are attuned to its thoughts as well as intuitions, fantasies, and other images, we are shown our personal wrongs as well as our good points (which are just as often ignored); we are shown how to take responsibility for our acts in very precise ways. The psyche longs to live out the purposes originating in the unconscious. To do so is to fulfill one's own destiny in the context of the world in the best way possible. The world desperately needs us to become more sensitive to our inner lives.

Desire plays an essential role in bridging conscious and unconscious factors in the psyche. The erotic desire to unite with another is in part a disguised longing for one to feel the wholeness of the psyche. To feel this wholeness an individual has to spend time and effort in contemplating the images that come from the psyche in an ongoing way. When one is successful in integrating and living their guidance, one will receive confirmation in dreams of union with Inner Lovers.

This is hardly an intellectual exercise. There is no getting around the fact that our bodies are the homes of our psyches, although people try to jump out of their skin in many ways. Through our physical senses we hear, smell, taste, touch, and see the world. With our bodies we make intimate contact with others. Our bodies hold the imprint of tensions, fears, joys, fatigue, excitement, and serenity. We've been too unaware of how the unconscious is expressed through the language of our bodies.

When we feel passionate desire for someone, we feel it physically. Our bodies can be giddy, pulsating, weak at the knees, or melted by the other's touch. When we are broken-hearted, our chests can feel crushed or twisted to the bone. When we experience both inner and outer union with lovers, we can feel sublime. Feelings flow through our body like the rainbow veils of the aurora borealis. All the dynamics of the Inner Lover journey take place on the field of our bodies. The inner marriage will be expressed in a bold body carried into the world.

But our lack of solid connection to Inner Lovers can readily be seen in situations when our stomachs clench or our throats clutch in fear at the prospect of speaking our feelings to another. How alarming vulnerability can seem! How we skirt our deepest desires! We are most afraid of what we want the most. Many of us are not able to face either the sharp blade that cuts away the old or the stretching of our hearts as they expand with the new. When our outer love bond brings pain, however, rather than turning hard with bitterness, we can take the attitude that we are being refined. When we surrender to being refined, we free up more vitality and compassion. When we refuse, we choose stagnation, and it will show up in a deadened, lusterless body.

Many of us have been deeply hurt in the past by not having received embraces, feeding, physical nurturance, and delight in our presences. We crave (and deserve) this attention and yet have most anxiety and defenses when it approaches. Attendance to Inner Lovers shows us how to heal this wound so that our psyches—body, mind, spirit—can be all they were meant to be.

Loneliness, Solitude, Suffering

Loneliness, solitude, and suffering are three fates that many of us think are awful. However, they are the very conditions that enable us to develop greater sensitivity to our inner landscape, to nurture the roots of desire, and to receive the riches of subjectivity. These can be the great soul builders, as long as one uses them constructively. Watching television to escape isolation is not the idea.

> and one day, . . . the woman says to the man,
> *I woke up feeling so sad this morning because I realized*
> *that you could not, as much as I love you, dear heart, cure my loneliness*
> —Robert Hass, "Privilege of Being"[3]

There are some paradoxes here.

Being alone does not have to feel lonely. Sometimes, as in the poem above, we know we have an incurable aloneness even when we are with another person. When we are feeling lonely, instead of rushing to seek anyone at all for relief, we can get comfortable with our own company.

A friend of mine who is a therapist said about her loneliness: "I have to come to terms with it over and over but I find over the years that I am not intimidated by it or thrown off course. Before, I used to get very frantic and have to call people. There was less of me then, and I was panicked by it. Loneliness has tempered me. It forces you to see what really sustains you. It's calmed me. It's given me a spine. I can be erect in it. It's given me insight into my personal and professional life. It's given me more compassion for people. And there's a part of me that is content with it, as when I am walking or sitting in a cafe or working on a paper."

In solitude we can explore the vicissitudes of a relationship and let our imaginations flow. The longing behind loneliness produces fantasies galore. We can see these as purposeful and not a waste of time.

Being alone with all the fantasies about one's beloved does not mean to be absorbed in them to the exclusion of real people. The beauty of solitude is that it enhances our outer bond as well as ourselves.

Absence versus presence is another paradox. We can experience distance from a lover because of quarrels or absence, but we know that distance is another form of presence. Some people will invent ways, even affairs, to create distance because of the need to experience what comes up in solitude. We feel the other more keenly because of being lonely. The attitude we take toward the obstacle that separates us from our beloved makes a big difference. Daring to face the abyss of loneliness silences the ego and makes room for the balancing activity of the unconscious.

It is well known that clinging to another hinders a relationship. In times of separation our energy stops flowing into outer activities and goes downward into our unconscious. Later on when I examine the Psyche-Eros myth, we will see that most soul growth takes place during the suicidal depressions over being separated, during which time projected images and instinctual forces are brought more fully into the light of consciousness.

Being in tune with all aspects of the psyche leads to wholeness, whether one is alone or with someone. But alone or in relationship one can feel empty. One has longings and is dissatisfied. The longings and wishes put one in touch with true desires, which inspire one to seek and find who or what one needs.

Emptiness and fullness are another paradox. When we are alone, we may feel empty. The emptiness is not because the person is not there, but because we are not alert to the presence of the Inner Lover. The Inner Lover helps us cope with emptiness because when we are with him or her, we feel fullness.

Suffering can cause us to try to shut down the inner flow. Over time, these contractions become little nuclei of larger patterns of avoidance. We develop an identity around them, an elaborate web of rationalizations about the way we are. Unfortunately these become self-fulfilling prophecies. Part of us is not happy with this situation. The part that feels dissatisfaction and pain is awake to what is really going on. Thus, going into and through our pain is healing.

Our psyche will try not to let us avoid the necessary suffering. It will inflict some dis-ease of the body or spirit until we pay attention. Awakening to the psyche, though, involves a different sort of suffering. It is the pain of yearning and stretching to be opened further. It may feel like a sick obsession but is a sign of inner movement and activity.

Here is how the anguish commonly goes: you love someone and suffer feelings of abandonment, fury, emptiness, and misery. Throughout the day fantasies come. He or she is pressing against your body, kissing you with longing, building toward union. The absence of the real lover makes you feel as if you are in an inferno, burning up. You make yourself work, clean, sleep. Your dreams are about him or her—day upon day, night after night. You are so consumed that you feel as though soon nothing will be left of you but ashes and smoke. He or she is not worth all this, you say. I must get on with my life. This isn't good for me.

If at this point we close the door on love, we are being premature. We must let our hearts be stretched open. People say they desperately want ecstasy but they do not leave themselves open to the intensity of their feelings long enough to receive it. They escape their feelings through drinking, working, exercising, or socializing compulsively. They experience depression, which is often just a black cloud of anxiety obscuring deeper meaning in life. Too often we don't go through the cloud to the clarity on the other side.

Fear though can be helpful to us by making us go slowly in a relationship, giving time and space to the erotic fantasies, bodily feelings, moods, and flights of fancy. We need time and patience to reflect on the meaning of what we say to each other. To do so is part of the passion in loving another's soul as well as our own. To be alert to what is happening inside ourselves and our beloved, without preconceived judgments, is to be "present."

Just as cooking food makes it easier to digest, so suffering breaks down our old attitudes and makes something new of us.

Meister Eckhart said, "Suffering is the fastest horse that carries you to perfection." Yielding to suffering is much more productive than resisting it. Herein is the true meaning of surrender and letting go. The value of surrender is in giving up and giving in to the changes taking place, going into the unknown, and allowing a new identity to emerge. When we yield to the presence of a nurturing Inner Lover, it is easier to let other people be who they are in all their differences and not oppress them with our demands.

Suffering must be long in order for transformation of the self to fully happen. Perhaps it is consoling to know that suffering has a helpful purpose behind it. For as past ways and attitudes are being dissolved, on another level new creative ideas and works are brought forth by these Inner Lovers. But the new cannot exist without the disintegration of the old. It may take months, years, decades of patience toward ur obsessions and tolerance of the heat/pain.

In this poem I describe how scary and exhilarating it can feel when the heart breaks . . . open:

My heart is breaking
You are here, there and elsewhere
my heart is breaking
my skin like a hot iron burns for you
my heart is breaking
I kiss your palm because I can't find the right words
my heart is breaking
my lips quiver like a child's whose mother is leaving
my heart is breaking
open to the depth of your voice

the lake in your crater, your hand on my breast
my heart is breaking
mice are nibbling at the cheese
snakes are slithering by
my heart is breaking
the hibiscus flared open today
the tomato is sun-warm and red
my heart is breaking
the dog is straining at the leash
the girl diving from the high board
my heart is breaking open
and rain is pouring in

Love as an Act of Imagination

James Hillman, a depth psychologist who writes frequently about the imaginal qualities of soul, said, "Love is mostly an explosion of imagination, an extraordinarily powerful way the psyche produces its images. Love seizes us, often takes us by surprise and shakes us violently."[4] When, at the beginning of an attraction, we are bombarded with fantasies, it is necessary to distinguish between our Inner Lover images from the personality of the other person as he or she is. Because these images continue whether or not we want them to, whether or not an outer relationship develops, we know that they are about our psychological development. It is as if they have a life of their own, an independent existence, that needs to be related to on its own terms.

In quiet reflection and solitude we can water the roots of our desires and fantasies and see how they are revealing our soul's purpose for us. Wishful thinking is ego-directed, while unbidden fantasies, which come from our unconscious, are well worth examining for messages. They strengthen our sense of reality because they show the possibly painful dark sides and subtleties that we tend to overlook.

People say they are most likely to be aware of fantasies before going to sleep or waking up. That is a twilight zone between sleeping and waking when one's conscious mind is less dominant and more open to the images and awarenesses from the unconscious.

Imaginal reality is just as important as social and physical realities. It's the key to creativity, healing, wholeness, holiness, and enterprise.

In infancy a child learns to hold an absent parent in mind as a solace. Sometimes it happens that a child's mother or father is absent through death or illness or some other reason, and that child will carry that parent in fantasy perhaps for the rest of his or her life. In a similar way we carry our Inner Lovers to support us.

Those who have been cut off from their fantasy life since childhood find that they have been missing a substantial part of life. Schools unfortunately cause many to lose confidence in their imaginal capacities. But, regardless, in everyone love will drive fantasies out of hiding. Love forces the ego to submit to deeper influences of the psyche.

Sexual fantasies are used by the psyche to show that they are about more than lust for an actual person. Men usually make a mistake not to see anything in their sex fantasies other than physical stimulation. But if they think again, they realize that the lovers in their fantasies wear certain clothes, are in particular places, and have certain expressions and gestures that add up to meaningful little stories.

Sometimes sexual fantasies develop toward a person in order to force us to relate to someone we would otherwise ignore. On the strength of these fantasies one overcomes the hesitancy to introduce oneself. Desire often arouses us out of stultifying torpor and isolation.

Ask: *What does my desire want of me?* One way to find out is to notice how we collect, heighten, or block the energy in our body, mind, or imaginative flow. We can let desire speak to us.

The space between desire and fulfillment, yearning and possessing, is imaginal. Here is where we feel the flow and force of Eros. Some say it is Eros itself that we want, more than we want the other person.[5] It's important at least not to identify Eros with the outer person. Eros is the warm glow of love that unites us with our souls, spawning protean images that will transmute us. The imaginal is a powerful and magical place.

The Interface of Passion, Psyche, and Creativity

Here is where our themes come together and find fulfillment. The Inner Lover journey is one that brings conscious and unconscious growth. In solitude and suffering we find that our Inner Lover images unfold purposefully and contribute to life.

Ethel S. Person, whose *Dreams of Love and Fateful Encounters* is a superb book about passion in its many nuances, says that no matter how messy, irrational, unstable, or ultimately unsuccessful love may be, it "is one of the most significant crucibles for growth" and is to be cherished whatever its outcome. It is easy to say that the treasures we find if we do surrender to the process are worth the struggles. The rewards are there, and we are meant to have them, but we must be willing to bleed emotionally. And who likes to bleed? It hurts, it's wet, it's fearsome because the razorcuts of love can leave scars. But when blood circulates freely through our veins, it carries nourishment. So it is with our emotions. Their coursing will lead us to passion and creativity in ever-renewing cycles of life.

Love is an adventure of the self, destination unknown. Our projections and disappointments can lead us to bountiful harvests as we integrate all that they mean to us. Here is a worthy passage from Ethel Person:

> In love we recover parts of the self. But we buried them only because they had brought us too much pain; either they led us to strive for the unattainable or belonged to the deep undifferentiated self. For example, the early wish that seeks satisfaction in the ecstatic oceanic sense of oneness with another must be buried if we are to differentiate and thrive as autonomous beings. It can come to the surface again—oh so tentatively—only in love or perhaps in religious transports. And when wishes as deep as this one find fulfillment, the exaltation we feel is extraordinary. The energy released when at last we feel loved and loving enough to admit our deepest needs, to allow those long buried parts of the self to surface, is what fuels the sheer exhilaration of love. The sense of relief and, ultimately, the peace with ourselves and with

the universe that we feel, is a result of coming to terms with our deepest feelings, finding in our beloved our "better half," that which we have previously repressed in ourselves. Ultimately, it isn't just the beloved with whom the lover identifies or the earlier images of the all-giving person or the "we"; the real discovery in love is the self What is most extraordinary about this recovery (and crucial to it) is that it can only occur when the lover makes all those other identifications so completely that he loses his usual inhibitions and forgets his narrow sense of self, and thus is enabled, ultimately, to find the larger self. This is the essential and defining paradox of love.[6]

Person describes how in infancy we possibly have our closest sense of oneness with our mothers, after which we grow up increasingly distant from others. Our falling in love reawakens that pleasurable primordial oneness. In the intimacy of sharing our subjective realities, we lessen the sense of separation. She writes, "We cannot begin to understand . . . love until we have understood that it's our deepest, oldest longings which find themselves fulfilled in it. It is because the wishes and feelings are from our very depths that the re-edition of them in romantic love is so intense and their fulfillment so profoundly exhilarating."[7]

Love, driven by passion, opens the pathways to our psyche; it is creative while *simultaneously* causing suffering. Abandoning ourselves totally to our love for another seems scary and (to those who are not in love) possibly crazy. But those who have done so know that there is wisdom in the chaos and risk. It turns out that in the longing to merge, one is not obliterated but enlarged.

Even if we find we are attracted to unsuitable others, our love gives us a chance to heal our childhood wounds in bits and pieces that we can handle. We don't need to condemn ourselves or others. The Self perpetually finds the ones in the world whom we need to help us grow.

As we become more aware of our Inner Lovers, we feel a better sense of our differences from each other and value that diversity. We are clearer about what belongs to ourselves and what belongs to the other, which frees up emotional intimacy. I had a dream that brought home this point: *I am with a man I love but am told that I can't have him until I don't have to go home with him.* My home is within me, not him. That sense of being at home with oneself is a major gift of the Inner Lover.

The more practice we have with the unfolding spools of love, passion, and creativity, the more vivid and vital the ego gets, and consequently able to withstand ever more powerful challenges and opportunities. Our personal issues become transparent to larger cultural problems. Things don't get better; they get deeper. Even if life seems one insult after another, our struggles do matter, because the larger unfoldment of the universe depends on how totally engaged we are.

Love is indeed a life or death matter, for it can add more life or subtract it. One can choose to surrender to being enlarged by love or else, by thwarting it, to being diminished. My hope with this book is to provide guideposts that make the journey more welcome in the good and bad times. In the despair of love, it can sometimes seem there are no possibilities.

But if one is attuned to one's subjective truths, one will be able to have a great adventure with love. For then one will experience the dynamics of love energy in one's soul. The benefits to one's outer relationships are enormous if one is in good rapport with one's Inner Lovers.

The emphasis of this book then is on what happens in the individual psyche from the enthusiastic explosion of fantasies at the onset of passion through the painful problems that arise. We need to get to know what's going on with our Inner Lovers as they appear and what they are trying to tell us and get us to accomplish in the world.

The next two parts, "Formative Years" and "The Many Lovers," show where the Inner Lover begins to form and how it is found in a variety of situations. The third part, "The Wedding," is about how union with the Inner Lover strengthens one's creative powers. The final part, "How to Use Inner Lover Fantasies," contains exercises which can be read before proceeding with the next parts, or they can be read and practiced after the contents have been digested. When I teach the Inner Lover concept, I introduce the exercises as we go, which is another way the reader can use them. The point is that the exercises can be done in whatever way the reader chooses. They are grouped at the end so that the reader can refer to them at will and continue to do them upon finishing the text.

PART TWO

Formative Years

Parents in Childhood and Adolescence

Aparent is a child's first lover, who leaves a lifetime imprint. Whatever one experiences at the hands of that person will surely have to be contended with when one grows up.

We all deserve to be loved and seen as precious but, of course, that does not happen consistently for any of us. We know that parental figures are often projected onto future partners. Even when we choose someone completely opposite from our parent, we are still caught in reacting against that parent.

The control can seem as inescapable as a steel vise or a foot on the back of the neck. Working with Inner Lovers can help free one from being controlled by the unconscious in that way.

Germaine Greer's recent book, *Daddy, We Hardly Knew You*, describes her search for the true details about her father's life. She writes, "That my father never once struck or reviled me was reason enough for me to love him," even though his favorite remark to her was "You're big enough and ugly enough to take care of yourself." Such stinginess with love becomes engrained and extends into what one expects in future partners. The authority and (perhaps false) heroic stature of a parent are equally difficult to buck. One wonders if Anna Freud, who was analyzed at the age of twenty-two by her father and thereafter led a celibate life, was

unable to have love bonds on her own because of being so sub-
sumed emotionally by her father. Such a tenacious grip on one's
psyche by a parent occurs even among those of us whose parents
are not famous, and even if we think we have escaped them by
moving far away.

Harshness or fear doesn't constrict so much as the fact that
our experience dictates what we define as love. When a child
seems to receive no love, he or she will fabricate the illusion of
love, perhaps as a way to get by. In this way painful situations are
experienced as love. We just don't know any better.

Anthony Storr in *Solitude* writes about boys who felt abandoned or orphaned by their mothers and consequently become
isolated or else highly defended against intimacy in bonds where
they could be hurt again. Robert Bly writes about how his mother
colluded with him against his alcoholic father, thereby forcing him
to be dependent on her and guilty for trying to leave. Some men
have felt so controlled by their mothers that they avoid intimacy
for fear of being trapped. Yet many men search for the primordial
oneness that they once experienced with their mothers. It comes
out in different guises. One man told me of his mother's chaos
seeming like the world's, which he wanted to reform. Many men
also lose the capacity for intimacy because of learning in childhood of their difference—hence, separation—from the female.

The most telling sign that a parental figure is poisoning our present love relationship is when we are in the midst of an argument.
The very common feeling of being hurt or not getting enough
attention is a holdover from the past. Another typical sign is inarticulateness. It is a result of feeling ashamed of one's feeling or
sensing that it's useless to express it. These painful states come
from having to repress feelings when growing up. They will be
duplicated when we are engaged in battles with our most intimate
partners. Recognizing their origins can help prevent them from
doing damage. Doing so takes vigilance.

To illustrate how a parent can influence love relations I will use
my own experiences in some detail. I do so in this and other chapters with the hope that readers will feel encouraged to reflect on
how their particular past circumstances impinge on the present.

The dominant trauma of my childhood was the divorce of my parents and the consequent absence and distance of my father, despite his trying to be with me as much as he could.

I was born in 1940, at the outbreak of World War II. My father's heritage was German; my mother's Danish. Both were from Chicago. The bombs exploded in my home as well as abroad. My mother was the only daughter of doting Republican, conservative parents. My father, who was thirteen years older than my mother, was from an immigrant family with five siblings. His loyalty during the war was severely tested. The arguments between him and my mother, I suspect, contributed much to their divorce when I was three.

My father was essentially practical and hardworking. Born in 1904, he was only nine when World War I raged, along with extreme anti-German sentiment in the United States. He had teachers who ripped out pages on the Germans from history texts. The denunciation of the Germans continued unabated through the Second World War. Hence, he became a loner at an early age. He was antisocial, wary of people, and susceptible to severe headaches and intestinal disorders, which eventually became the colonic cancer that killed him at the age of seventy-three.

He must have felt his marriage to my mother as full of promise, however brief it turned out to be. He thought her beautiful and vivacious. She was much more extraverted than he. Together they engaged in somewhat of a social life, playing bridge and golf or tennis with friends. But then came the war, and he could not hate Germany properly. His parents had spoken German; they had relatives in Germany with whom they visited and corresponded. I think part of him even wanted to fight for Germany (known to Germans as *das Vaterland*—the Fatherland), despite the fact that he was the quintessential American as well—one who hitchhiked across the country, slept in fields, drove the first Ford, and watched baseball. My more conventional mother would have been horrified by his lack of patriotism.

Their divorce detonated in me for decades, and I often felt broken into shards. The divorce proceedings were nasty, as I later learned coming across a newspaper article about them in my grandfather's desk. He caught me reading it and snatched it out of my hand, and no explanation was given.

It was determined that I was to be separated from my mother and younger sister for six months and given to my father. My father later claimed this was part of my mother's strategy to prove him unfit to take care of me. Because my father had to work all day, he left me with his sister, who was married and at that time had one child. He would see me in the evening, but I am sure not for long, as at that age I must have gone to sleep early. Apparently he fought for custody but lost. In the end the arrangement was that my sister and I would live with my mother and her parents and spend every other weekend with my father. At one point my father didn't find that enough time and negotiated another weekend a month. We also spent the month of August with him.

Thus, the dominant motif of my life—longing for my father—was set into motion. He was the distant one, the idealized one, the one who could save me if only he were there, the one I pined and prayed for long after I grew up. And this image I had of him was the first manifestation of the Inner Lover. Of course, I didn't know it then. His being the first man in my life made all the difference.

My love for him was a little flame I kept alive by knowing that fortunately Daddy at least wanted to be with me, even though he wasn't physically there. Every Friday after work he picked us up at my mother's and grandparents' apartment until we were old enough to travel by bus to his office, where he ran a correspondence law school single-handedly (the better to be unbothered by other people, I think). He had a suit for each day of the week. His shoes were always polished. He was about five feet eleven, slender, and wore wire spectacles over his blue eyes. His lips were full but drawn tight. His forehead was creased, making him look serious and thoughtful. Then I considered him noble. His set, determined ways were proof of his integrity. Whenever we were with him, my father did not include other women.

This remarkable fact made me proud, but it actually is rather strange. He did not marry again until after my sister married, about ten years after I had. When we were children there was only one Christmas that he included another woman, the mother of a friend of ours. She came with us to our cousins' and was an awkward presence in our games. Once, when she must have thought they were alone, I saw her kissing him; he was blushing in a way I'd never seen. I was quite annoyed. That romance—the only one I was ever aware of—didn't last long.

Thus, as a young child I did not have to compete with a grown woman for my father's attention. He was quite willing to give it all to me and my sister. Even though he was a divorced father, I received a lot from him in certain ways. However, I was very much deprived of the reality of a day-to-day relationship.

Daddy held my hand when we walked around the city. I sat in his lap when he read to me. He carried me on his shoulders and would jump on the bed, throwing me down deliriously laughing. At night he told us stories as we lay in the dark.

He had lofty plans about educating us in an elite manner. When I was six, he enrolled me in a private girls' school in Evanston. Vassar or Wellesley was to be the next step. I believe he would have preferred it if we never grew up, but if we had to, the only way we would succeed would be by marrying well. Early on he started us off on riding lessons.

For a while I had a mysterious fever, for which I was even hospitalized. I believe this fever was a deep reaction to the conflict between my parents. The only visitor I recall was Daddy, who came with a doll I had wanted.

Time spent with my father was much more satisfying than with my mother. He bought me books and coats and hats with grosgrain ribbons hanging down the back. He taught me how to ride a bicycle and to catch fireflies and play softball. Summer evenings we'd get rainbow cones or have "black cows." I never tired of hearing him recite "Wynken, Blynken, and Nod" as we were walking at night under a canopy of stars. His mother, a soft, dimpled, white-haired woman, taught us how to knit and to bake banana cake, our favorite dessert. She made clothes for my dolls. As I got older, Daddy would cook simple dishes with me at home. In this way I learned more domestic arts from him than from my mother. One day I told Daddy I wanted to marry someone just like him. He said later I would get different ideas. I didn't believe him and told him he could pick out my husband. I couldn't understand his laughter.

But then another bomb dropped when I was eleven. One Sunday afternoon my father brought us back to the apartment as usual, but this time instead of closing the door on him, my mother invited him in for a talk. She was tense. He stiffened. I buried my face behind the newspaper and pretended not to be there. My mother announced that she was marrying a man from Texas and would be moving us there. During that conversation I learned that earlier on she'd wanted to marry but my father talked her out of it because of us. This time he couldn't. Nevertheless, he said he would fight to block her from moving us. I hated her for doing this to us. She was taking us away from Daddy. It was too cruel.

A legal battle ensued. This one I remembered all too well. The tension sickened me. One time Mother and Daddy almost came to blows. My grandparents kept after me about loving my mother and going to Texas without complaint. My mother raved about how wonderful Texas was and how evil my father was. My father attempted to be more philosophical about my getting through rough times.

At no time during my childhood did either of my parents talk to me about my hurt feelings about their divorce or why we lived the way we did. The topic was surrounded with silence. I was taught to be good and quiet. Expressions of anger, sadness, or criticism were swiftly squelched. I learned to keep everything to myself and was afraid to bring up anything that might upset them. My will was subordinated to theirs without hesitation. This is the conditioning I would bring to future relationships, which later contact with Inner Lovers helped to change. (While the lives of others may differ in the details, many of them share the same emotional results.)

One day in court we were brought into the judge's private chamber. He asked me if I loved my mother. By then that was a rote question, and I answered yes automatically. The judge said he didn't see why we shouldn't live with her. And that was that. My father and I embraced in the hallway as if we were being separated forever.

Texas. I resented going from the beginning to the end. The first summer we knew no one and had nothing to do. It was beastly hot. I sulked. The public school was terrible. It seemed a long, long wait until Christmas before I could go back to my father.

The pain of separation from my father made it impossible for me then to realize that if I did live side by side with him, I might chafe at his limitations, as kids do in order to become separate and leave home. My consciousness just got very accustomed to longing. It was a coping mechanism then but also the beginnings of imaginative flow. I fell back on it like a computer reverting to its default mode. On the waves of longing came fantasies of comfort and safety and love. In my mind I carried his love for me. Through these fantasies I nurtured myself through the difficult days. In this way I learned one of the positive functions of the Inner Lover—that is, imagining love, letting it flower and heal.

Throughout my childhood, while I never had to compete with my mother for my father's attention, I did have to contend with her constant jealousy of and anger at my focus on him. Although her hurt and rage often went unexpressed, it was powerfully present between us. Once in Texas she read my diary, which had a number of entries about missing my father. She erupted in a tirade against me when I came home from school. The way I responded was to shield my true feelings from her and to try to appease her as much as possible.

People often speak in a flat tone about horrible events that have happened to them, because their psyches go into shock and are numbed to agonies and terrors of separation, beatings, abandonments, and other abuses. Sometimes it takes therapy or years of painstaking awareness before those numbed parts get feeling back again. So it was with my relation to the divorce between my parents. I had cut off my mother as being just too difficult to bear. This turning aside from her was a habit I developed that made it difficult for me to be really close to anyone. I did not know how people expressed love or need or just relaxed into someone. I once watched with an aching heart a friend's child go back and forth to her lap all afternoon. The mother's body was a warm secure haven. If as a child one learns that warmth and security are there for the asking, as an adult one can trust to find it in other people. Many of us do not have that faith.

I often wondered about what my father did all those months when I was in school in Texas. All I knew was that he lived alone, worked, and played golf. Rarely did he go on a vacation. He wrote us letters twice a week and called once a week. There was no mention of women friends. Sometimes from my bed at night I would look at the moon and think he could be looking at it too and that at least was a connection.

When we were with him in the summer, he devoted all his nonworking time to us. He began teaching us tennis and golf diligently with daily practice sessions. He bought us a horse. While he was at the office, we cleaned and shopped, rode our horse, and played tennis. At night after our practice sessions with him, the three of us would go home, cook dinner, play cards, or read. Sometimes when I'd be alone scrubbing down the bathroom tiles, I'd fantasize that I was my father's wife. In my mind I was "married" to him, and I liked having that special place, just as I'm sure he must have unconsciously wanted me in it.

When I was fifteen, my father decided to leave his new Ford Thunderbird with me, after he drove us from Chicago to Texas at the end of the summer. It was typical of my father to leave me with something grand while he had nothing.

The night after he'd left and my sister and I were unpacking, adjusting to the transition from father to mother, my mother took an overdose of phenobarbital and collapsed on the kitchen floor. I found her. She'd left a note blaming my stepfather. He called an ambulance. She was in the hospital for a week, while my sister and I waited in bewilderment. When she came home, she looked tired and defeated and sad. Neither then nor at any later time did she or we speak about why she had attempted to kill herself. I had much submerged guilt and anger toward her.

But the car gave me a great deal of unexpected freedom.

In high school years life for me in Texas with my mother was very different from life in Chicago. My mother liked boys and urged me to follow suit, while at the same time her second husband gave me lectures about virginity. In Texas I did not stay home evenings but went around with my friends and did have a number of boyfriends. But during summers in Chicago my father enforced the circle of three (him, my sister, and me) with silent coercion. He did not permit us to drive around, spend evenings out, or have independence.

In Chicago once I had a crush on a college boy, whose fierce way of playing tennis impressed me. One day he asked me out for a date to a concert. There was no way I was not going to go but I felt I could not just simply say yes. I was scared of my father's reaction.

The date that should have been so exciting turned out to be a miserable event. The way I handled it was to tell Bill that he should pick me up at a friend's, where I said I was spending the night. My plan was to be in front of the friend's house and to go home on my own, without either my friend or father knowing. I told my father I was spending the evening with my friend. As fate would have it, it rained, and Bill called me at home to say he would be late. By then I was gone, and my father answered the phone and learned about my lie. When Bill picked me up, he told me what had happened, so for the whole evening I knew that my father knew I'd lied to him, and that was all I could think about. When I arrived home, my father was lying in bed awake in the dark. He said curtly, "We'll talk in the morning."

At breakfast I apologized and explained. I said I wanted to go out with Bill again. We established that I would, which is how it came to be that I could go out on dates when I was with my father. But the sorrow that hung around this event was thick and lasting.

Thus I remained Daddy's girl even when I was with other boys. In Chicago I did not desert our circle more than several times during a summer.

At college I met the man I would marry. When my father learned of my seriousness about him, he offered to finance a year in Europe after college. I declined that because I knew he was just trying to make me not think of marrying.

Although my father did not know it, I wanted to fulfill a vow I'd made to myself from the time I'd been torn from him in childhood. That goal was to return to my father after college and live with him in a daily way, as I had been unable to do ever since my mother had left him. I'd dreaded telling my mother that I chose to live with my father rather than her, because it would hurt her. But I did just that, and after college returned to Chicago and got a job. My father and I rode the subway downtown together and often had dinner together, just like a couple. But the timing was wrong. This existence was as dry as cornstalks in autumn. My will, plus a hidden mountain of fear, would not let me leave my father though.

It took becoming pregnant to take me away. In retrospect, I believe the life instincts of the unconscious came to my rescue. When I told my father I was pregnant, I trembled, although I was secretly glowing about the conception of this baby. He said I would have to get married. Other than give me a car for driving East, he participated in no other way. He did not host nor attend my marriage, nor my sister's years later. He offered no words of hope or fear or sorrow. I, the delight of his eye as a child, had grown and left him. I accepted his remoteness as the way things were, not reflecting until years later that he never said he loved me nor that it must have been as hard for him to let me go as for me to leave him.

Although I had literally left my father's house, psychologically he was imbedded in my mind. As an Inner Lover, he carried the image of being loyal, responsible, and financially generous (all his money was spent on my sister and me, not himself). I also constantly tried to please him and get his attention, while at the same time unknowingly suffering from his inability to express his love or support of my instinctual femaleness and creativity. I would go through other relationships in which I was not "seen" without even realizing it, just hurting in an old familiar way. Gradually I gained the courage to expect more from others and also to give more.

The way I saw my father in childhood was different from the way I experienced him in adulthood. Because he was so important an ideal to me as I grew up though, it would be a long time before any future lover would be able to replace him in my psyche.

Parents in Adulthood

How does the image left over from a parental figure interfere with outer relationships after you have grown up? The problem lies within one's own psyche where the fantasies are holdovers from the past. The first step in combating the problems lies in recognition of the symptoms.

Think of your own childhood experiences and the images you formed of your mother and father and how you interacted with them. Compare them with other bonds you've formed. Did any of your parents' qualities show up in later relationships or did you deliberately seek what a parent lacked? What are your most common emotional reactions when you are in conflict with a lover?

Sometimes men and women will back off from intense relationships because they fear reexperiencing pain that has its roots in childhood. People fend off intensity with a variety of excuses. They are suspicious that they are being tricked. Or, there is something wrong with them that they could feel so dependent on another. As a result of these fears, they grow bored and listless about life. Yet, when such people are encouraged to trust and yield to their feelings, they are surprised at how much zest and animation they regain.

Ann Ulanov writes in *Receiving Woman*: "A woman may project onto a man the qualities of a supportive, loving father she never had. Eventually she must claim this supportive energy for herself in herself, lest she remain a sort of father's daughter all her life, transferring to teacher, to employer, to political figure, whomever, this dynamic image she feels so much in need of. To recover a conscious connection to this support entirely within herself would free her from a fixed daughter role, free her to claim a secure inner authority, and to grow up into full womanhood."[1]

A woman who had been squashed by her father intellectually had a dream, after a long process, in which he appeared humbly naked before her. For her this was a turning point; she became much more confident in her outer life.

One way a woman compensates for her own timidity is to blame men for exactly what she is afraid of doing. Thus, she sees men as weak, frightened of her emotions, easily blown over, always interpreting her actions and attitudes as demanding. Such a woman probably turns away from her own passion. She will have to overcome a habit of silence and doubt and learn with the help of compensating Inner Lovers to affirm what she feels.

A woman dreams of her lover coming into her house. She acts like a geisha girl for him and then is not happy with their intercourse. In discussing the dream she at first blamed the man, until she realized that she was too passive and just eager to please. If she asserted her own desires more, she would be more fulfilled.

In my case, my father had shown me some good qualities about men. His loyalty, discipline, and sportsmanship were certainly admirable and useful. But the way I idealized him ended up having a negative effect for it lured me away from my outer lover-husband.

Although I had longed to be close to my father, I did so by learning to restrain myself in dress, sex, talk, and writing. In dreams Inner Lovers would show the cruelty of this habit and how it extinguished my passion. Eventually my Inner Lovers would turn despair and hunger into peace and contentment. The journey would be marked by the changing image of my father in dreams. As I became more psychologically aware, he turned from being an authoritarian giant to an ordinary helper. But first I had to witness the destructive side of the Inner Lover as it worked through me in my relationships.

One of the most pronounced examples was the way I would be involved with men who were uncomfortable with my intense feelings, just as Ann Ulanov describes above, and I would have to reclaim my passion. But when I married my husband, I was not at all aware of this challenge. He was spontaneous and clownish, everything my father was not, which was delightful to me.

A day or two after Brian and I had gotten married, we were in a motel. Brian was showering. He'd been smiling, animated, and happy about this new venture in his life. I should have been too. But I was lying on the bed, picking at the spread, thinking with melancholy about my father. Brian came out of the shower, a towel jauntily tied at his waist, combing back his hair, eager to talk. My moroseness dampened the mood. This was a representative moment. My father was a shadow between us. Despite my thinking I was on my own and had chosen my own man, I was inexorably tied to my father's attitudes and behavior. I had not separated cleanly nor fully placed my respect in my husband. I thought I loved Brian but later I realized that in my psyche he had not displaced my father. In the moment with Brian I was only aware of a souring of the atmosphere between us.

At age twenty-one I would have even denied it if someone pointed out to me that I didn't put Brian first. Hadn't I been thrilled with our opportunity to live away from family in France for three years? My father came over to visit twice—the first time with my sister to visit our newborn daughter. The second time I was urging him to come in order to visit his parents' families in Germany. Since he'd often spoken proudly of his heritage, I was glad to be the catalyst for bringing about a reunion. While I was enthusiastic, he went through it stiffly. I was disappointed but even more so by the drive back from Germany to France. Brian stopped at a particularly picturesque village and wanted to stroll about. I would have been glad to go along with Brian. But my father fumed. Can't we just keep going? We'll never get there at this rate. I was furious at my father for being so impatient but dreaded a scene. I literally felt torn between both men and could not make a move. My father's petulance angered Brian, who drove the rest of the way, peeved.

The conflict between the two raged inside me. I fought to keep it hidden rather than express anything. I felt isolated from both of them.

My marriage did not change the weekly letter writing or phone calls between my father and me. I was determined not to let it. I would not abandon my father, even if I just relayed news about outer events to him and little of my own thoughts. I also took the children—often not Brian—back to Chicago to visit him in order to reunite us. With Brian along we'd have to stay in a separate apartment and then I would not feel I was home. I felt tense when the two men were together. Yet my father took no special interest in teaching my children sports the way he had me. I eventually stopped bringing my children on visits to him. It was easier to go by myself.

We spoke of none of these matters. On one visit I had a dream that *he is holding my hand as we stand facing the vast breadth of Lake Michigan. He says that I am to cross that water, but he is afraid to let go of my hand.* Undoubtedly he himself could not let go of me either, a desire that remained unconscious and could only come in a dream to me. At the time I was not sure what to do with it.

Like many women (and men in regard to their mothers), I saw my father as a beloved, whom I betrayed for another man. Until his death I felt guilty.

One time I'd become angered and upset over his calling Brian an "asshole" in front of me. I wrote him a three-page letter that I never sent. Then in my usual monotone letter but with my fingers trembling violently over the keys, I suggested that he must have had indigestion when he made the remark about Brian.

After worrying for a week about my father's reaction to my "daring," I received his usual call. He didn't mention my letter. Nor did I. I was terrified of getting recognition from him for my real feelings. I was sure he wouldn't love me.

I regret this painful inarticulateness so much. Yet overcoming it has been a long, fearful battle for years. Once on a visit I wanted to dare to ask him about his relationship with my mother, a topic we'd never discussed as adults. For an hour before I was to broach the subject on a long car ride, I was so anxious that I paced around a park for an hour, actually wringing my hands. I did manage to ask the question but I couldn't keep the conversation going. He made a derogatory statement about her and sex and skipped to his present wife. I didn't find out anything of note. Searching reflectively for meaning or understanding was not something we ever did nor did I know how to do it aloud with him.

He remained single until 1973, when at the age of seventy he married the widow of his best golf buddy. He used to admire this woman—she was blond, blue-eyed, pretty, and loyal. I thought he saw her as an angel. At first I had to adjust to his being taken away by another woman. I did not think she would fulfill his expectations as I did. But then I became disgusted by ways he would deride or ignore her.

After starting to do psychological work on myself, I began to realize the lack of intimacy I'd had with my parents and husband. I also became bolder and freer in my behavior. For example, on a visit to Chicago, I made arrangements to visit two friends in addition to my father, something I would not have dared to do before, even though I had wanted to badly. One woman had been the editor of my first book as well as an editor for Anaïs Nin, and the other I'd also come to know through Anaïs Nin. Both represented a new erotic freedom and creative magic that so charmed me. Without my father's knowledge, I also tried indulging myself for a night with a black poet I'd met in New York City. However, despite my gaining a measure of freedom, when the actual night came, I could not relax. In the forefront of my mind was how I was deceiving my father. The event was too reminiscent of the time I'd lied in order to go out on a date years before. I was much relieved when the evening ended and I could go back to being a good girl rather than a bad woman again. Of course, not least of my fears was the awareness that my father would probably kill me if he knew I was with a black man.

I was severely upset when I knew I would have to announce to my father that Brian and I would probably divorce. My father expressed no sympathy, only criticism. I felt guilty. I did not realize then that my feelings had been ignored. One doesn't notice if it is the norm.

My nineteen-year-old marriage to Brian and my father's life came to an end at the same time. Brian was never to know me free of the spectral influence of my father. My father's final decline coincided with the year Brian and I were separated and painfully enduring divorce negotiations and upheavals. For me I was losing the two major male presences in my life.

Ironically I was not able to be with my father when he died. The likelihood of his death had gone undiscussed; it came sooner than I had expected. I was in California on a job interview and arrived at the hospital one half-hour after the fact. My plane had been one half-hour late in getting off.

I was left alone with him for as much time as I wanted but I did not stay long. His body was stretched out in the hospital bed. His hands were carefully folded above the sheet. The lines in his face were smoothed out as if all interior pain had vanished. I felt there was nothing to say then and I didn't cry. I touched his chest, stroked his still warm head and hands, even kissed him, aware I was fondling him more than I would have if he were alive. I was reminded of being a little girl and wanting to touch him freely.

For days I felt grief, loyal to the lost absent love. He was imbedded in my bones. He is part of the clothes I wear, the body I bring to others for better or worse. In time I became more myself and dropped habits maintained because of him. The first appurtenance to fall away was golf. Then I stopped playing tennis, as after a divorce that was an expendable expense.

My adulation of my father had been so predominant that I, like many others, have needed a long phase of being aware of how he failed me in order to bring him into proper perspective. Above all, there was the lack of playfulness, spontaneity, and eroticism. He repressed these elements in himself (probably due to his own upbringing) and chewed them out in me.

I had a dream in which *Helen wants to give him and me a present.* (She was a close friend who represented unrestrained exhibitionism or flamboyance.) *She is late for dinner, and Daddy starts eating without her, refusing to wait or grant her any importance. I am upset*

41

that she'll be hurt and equally afraid to anger my father by requesting he wait. The dream shows how I wanted both to recognize the Helen side and also appease the side of restraint and criticism. It was a sign I had not yet broken free of my father's control.

A parent can dominate one's psyche very tenaciously, as my father did mine, despite one's wishes. It may take years of psychological work to unbind yourself. Even so, old attitudes will creep into situations. You will be better able to recognize them and weed them out before they take over as you pay attention to dreams. Noting dreams is the most important step you can take toward accessing help from the unconscious.

Also, when you have learned to recognize positive Inner Lover figures you can use them to counteract repressive, limiting, harsh feelings left over from the past. You can actually call upon your Inner Lovers to help you be more courageous in letting down the barriers to intimacy. A man I know, for instance, calls upon the women inside him who are tender, friendly, and nurturing, to help him relate to people's concerns better. Doing so counteracts his usual reaction of feeling hostile if attacked. Events turn out much better for him.

The foregoing has been a mapping of my father's power in my psyche. As it has been for me, the imprinting of your parents will lay the groundwork for you. But fortunately there are other influences to take us away from our parents in order to add essential qualities to our beings.

Love Buds

As we have seen, the contract formed between us and our parents will be the model for future relationships. We will blame others for evoking in us past hurts. There is nothing we can do about the way our past can poison our present until we start becoming more aware of how the imprint of our childhood affects the way we respond to new people. Remembering is healing, so letting our memories and reveries speak to us helps.

Our early ventures out of the family nest also greatly influence our budding selves. The passage will be carried along by our intense feelings for a teacher or a camp counselor and, of course, others closer to our age. As adults, we can pay attention to these experiences when memory and dreams bring images to consciousness. Writing them down with as much of the sensory details as possible helps stimulate awareness of the time.

Our youthful crushes are rehearsals for our fuller love attachments. They enable us to feel those physical fibrillations and tormenting attempts to get near the subjects of our attention. They are our first try since early infancy to reach out for intimate love.

In sixth grade I had a big crush on a boy named Buddy. The closest I ever got to him were the times he and I were the finalists in a spelling contest and when he was my partner at our first formal dance. All my palpitations over him far exceeded the outer connection. I am sure I had my mother drive by his house many many times. Did he ever think of me? I'll never know, for I did not speak to him of my feelings.

How many of us do? Don't we all identify with the blushing, stammering fool in so many jokes, because of having been there? Perhaps we confide our secrets to one special friend, or keep somewhat of a distance by only speaking to our heart's object on the phone. Phone calls themselves can be fraught with heart swings and pauses laden with dread and excitement.

In an article about children's crushes in the *New York Times*, psychologist Lawrence Kutner wrote:

> This type of crush occurs as children are beginning to accept the idea that they will eventually leave home and cease receiving their parents' day-to-day care. They are looking for ways to try out new forms of intimacy. Rather than rushing into face-to-face intimate relationships, preadolescents search for ways to take half steps. . . .
>
> . . . having a crush gives children an opportunity to rehearse some of the feelings they expect to have when they're older, and to put some of their fears in perspective. . . . The essence of a crush is that the relationship is fantasy.[1]

In adolescence we enter new territory. We are no longer babes. We have been children, each of us caught in a particular family drama. We are hungry for more love and go beyond our initial family in our search. Our bodies are urgent and experimental. In accepting our impulses, trying out styles of behavior, getting to know different people, fantasy and imagination are busily engaged.

Many of our early connections are played out mostly in our imaginations but are important for the future. We are setting forth on a great adventure. We will be shy, awkward, afraid, and bold with various successes and failures. It is a time when our behavior with another may be awkward but our feelings passionate. Undoubtedly our hearts will be broken, which means we will taste the salty tears of things not working out the way we wanted them to. At such crucial points we risk doing violence to ourselves or others. Many men and women can trace to adolescent disappointments their inner decision to shy away from intimacy.

Defending against future bruises by turning away from our intensity and fantasy life eventually takes its toll. Our youthful romances test our resiliency in staying open to others and learning what life has to teach us through them. Nothing less than who we are becoming as persons is at stake.

Stars

Onto the adolescent stage appear stars: film stars, music stars, mythical heroes from Lancelot to Wonder Woman. For an adolescent, stars can be the focus of unleashed fantasies without any of the limits imposed by actual relationship. Generally no one will ever speak face to face with a rock or movie star. The conversations we have in our imaginations are of importance though. Stars are blatant, rather crude examples of sexual styles. They appeal to us because we are young in our development. Subtler shadings appeal later on when we are ready for more complexity.

When I was fifteen, the star for me was Elvis Presley. I got closer than is customary to the catalyst in that I actually talked to and even kissed him, but my experience illustrates how the dynamic of the Inner Lover works in regard to famous people.

The setting: small Texas town . . . 1955 . . . riding around with my friends in the aquamarine Thunderbird convertible . . . school . . . smoking . . . dancing to a jukebox in a place called the Doghouse . . . kissing in musty old cars by the lake out of town . . . the scary tantalizing thrill of arousal in my body.

At this juncture Elvis Presley was nineteen years old. He had left Tennessee and hooked up with two musicians, Sonny and Scotty, and begun touring Texas to perform wherever they could, mostly in school auditoriums. He was just a young aspirant like many others. He lived with his mother and father and had a girlfriend. The conjunction of his life with girls (and eventually boys) like us around the country was electric, and soon he would be known in history. This is how I met him.

One night in the parking lot of Son's City Pig (the town café), a level-headed girl who had always seemed not to like boys told me about this boy wonder she'd seen sing in Abilene the night before. I perked up and decided to go see him when he came to sing later in our high school auditorium. Never before had I been to see a singer.

Elvis was no doubt the first singer to inspire the "groupie" phenomenon among infatuated teenagers that has continued with the Beatles, Prince, and other rock idols. When Elvis appeared on our stage, he looked like a sensuous Adonis, dressed from head to foot in ivory white—shoes, pants, soft shirt with loosely rolled cuffs. His hair was slightly askew, giving him a boyish look that made him seem one of our generation. Most surprising and captivating was a shy but sexy smile that would come over him laconically. He seemed at times to suddenly become aware of himself standing before us. His grin then was like saying, "This is really embarrassing, I'm not like this." But then he would get absorbed in the bluesy rhythms of the song, and he would smile out of oneness with the music. His gutsy, throbbing, heartrending voice thrilled us through and through.

In those days he was singing "That's All Right, Mama," "Blue Moon of Kentucky," "Baby Let's Play House." When he rumbled throatily, many of us swooned (it just happened). After the program I along with others went backstage and got him to scribble his name on paper. That scrap seemed a trivial substitute for the real person but in the asking for it we greeted him, and he got to know our faces, which he later told us was important to him.

He spent that night, along with his musicians, in a motel just outside of town and rumor had it the next morning that he was eating breakfast at a diner. Another friend and I went down there. When he saw us, he invited us to sit down. The five of us laughed and talked, and that is how it seemed to me Elvis and his friends were like other school kids (I don't think he ever outgrew this stage). Afterward my friend scooped Elvis's toast crusts off his plate and took them home with her.

We were so excited by him that we had to do more than talk to each other, so some of us ventured out to the local radio station. The disk jockey there told us how Elvis had stopped by with his latest 45 record. We breathily discussed Elvis's every word and every detail of his clothes. The disk jockey suggested we start a fan club for him. We could get Elvis to sign cards and offer his photograph. That seemed like a great idea as well as a project we could handle. That a real grownup thought we could do it must have been part of the excitement.

So the first creative result of Elvis Presley as our Inner Lover was this fan club. It emerged because we needed a place to put our excess energy.

We set up officers and found out how to design and print a membership card. We drafted notices and contacted Elvis about getting us photographs. When we next saw Elvis sing in another town, we went out to eat with him, while he signed one hundred cards. In such small ways, duplicated in many states, his fame spread far and wide. It cost twenty-five cents to join the club. I used to be amazed at the letters that came in from women who would describe their measurements, as if proffering themselves to Elvis via us.

We were ecstatic at the opportunities we had to see Elvis before he became nationally famous and almost inaccessible. The few times we had together, Elvis acted glad to see us. He recognized us and welcomed us backstage for short visits. He flirted, kissed our young mouths, and thoroughly delighted us.

Between visits we played his records again and again, memorizing every word, pause, breath, and chuckle. (In this way I, like many others, kept him very present, while paradoxically in fact he was absent.) I would lie on my bed, listening and dreaming so much that my mother threatened to take the records away. I talked her out of it. But her reaction was typical of the way others react on seeing an obsession they do not share. The boys at school were angry, and they jealously tried to spread belittling rumors about him (just as others would do so later in print). I described Elvis to my father as the Bing Crosby of our generation, thinking that that desexed explanation would pacify him. (Here was an example of how afraid I was to be forthright with my father about sex.)

I was consumed by romantic passion for Elvis even though he was inaccessible. The songs—for instance, "Heartbreak Hotel"—were about the tortures of love and longing. Elvis sang them with his whole body. His fervor was a flame to my body. On my fantasy screen I replayed his mobile body and smile. He would look bemused and then curl his upper lip, or he would purse his lips and shake his forelock. His skin seemed to tremble with rhythm. When his knee jiggled, culminating in arm and leg thrusts, I pulsated along with him. My favorite song was "Tryin' to Get to You." It was about "traveling over mountains, baby, trying to get to you" and expressed trying to bridge the gap between him and me—between the lover and beloved.

As part of my aroused passion, I tried to interest Elvis in me. The letter I wrote him is a mixture of trying to tell him everything about my young life, in an extreme self-conscious and tittering way, and trying to be clever and enticing. Whereas other girls thought their measurements would suffice, I apparently hoped other aspects would appeal. But Elvis was catching the wave of big-time fame and fortune and was being carried far away. Soon too he was going to be in the army in Germany, where he would take up with the fourteen-year-old Priscilla. When I heard that, I did not think my attempts were so far-fetched.

My adolescent obsession with Elvis, then, aroused a great deal of fun and excitement through singing and dancing. It did not, however, prevent me from having a wonderful boyfriend, who pretended to ignore the flap over Elvis.

At seventeen I left my world in Texas behind and went off to college in Massachusetts. Over the next two decades I was not much interested in Elvis. When he came back from Germany, he made a string of movies in which he sang songs that were pallid compared to the raunchy ones of his early days. I noted how Priscilla left him so she could have her own life, and I didn't like his trying to keep her imprisoned at Graceland. I saw his comeback attempts and the assorted hair colors and styles and costumes. I did not like his manager's way of treating him like a circus act. I didn't buy his recordings except for a few that captured the old fire, including the spirituals "When You Walk Through a Storm" and "How Great Thou Art."

And then suddenly in 1977 he was dead. The sadness I felt about his fate made me resurrect my scrapbooks of memorabilia and write a book proposal that was accepted by Atheneum Publishers. Writing this book gave me time to re-immerse myself in Elvis' songs and qualities. Thus, in addition to the fan club, another tangible outcome of my love for Elvis was a book.

This is an example of how the Inner Lover creates. One has feelings and fantasies that are embodied by the image of an Inner Lover. In time this exciting and pleasurable experience manifests through creative experiences that can give others pleasure as well.

Elvis continues to have an impact on my inner life and style. I will occasionally play his music and dream about him, enjoying the facets of my projection onto him. As I said in one of my dreams, "I like liking Elvis."

He has appeared in different guises in my dreams. In one, he was very heavy and depressed. He had an illness around his throat and ear. This image suggested to me some ways in which I was not able to hear or express my feelings. Expression of the heartfelt has been a long struggle for me. Well into my forties, I have felt mute. In one dream I was in the bathtub with him and Henry Miller. Henry Miller also represents bold, sexy expression. Elvis' appearance in my dreams reminds me to express myself much more animatedly.

Such is my story. Who are the stars that have attracted you? We all project fantasies onto stars. Movie stars, singers, authors, athletes, and even political heroes are ideal for this kind of projection. The list of examples over the decades is legion: Cary Grant, Jack Kerouac, Marilyn Monroe, Sally Ride, Madonna, John F. Kennedy, Tom Seaver, and Martha Graham are just a few. One reason we like movies so much is that we like going into the dark and letting our fantasies unfurl.

Many of us have favorite cartoon figures that we have dreamed of being like, for example, Miss Fury, Brenda Starr, Little Lulu, Dick Tracy, Superman. Harbored in the hearts of many a fan of baseball, boxing, tennis, and track are plans to imitate and compete. Through fantasy, sport heroes inspire and motivate.

It has often been said that women are turned on by power precisely to the degree that they lack it themselves, and thus they will idolize men and try desperately to get near them. Standing in the light of the man, they hope they will get some for themselves. (Ironically, the man of power often has less time or energy available to give to love than an average guy.)

While females swarm and swoon in ways that males don't, men's secret fantasies are just as strong as women's—they pin up centerfolds. Men often think that they are just sexually attracted to a star, but usually the attraction has a soul component as well. Take Marilyn Monroe. On the surface she was a sex goddess for many men. But she also had a soft vulnerability that most men completely lack and need to develop. For a man to not realize this is to limit his potential.

We frequently hear of the problems caused by men and women not seeing each other as they really are. A man reminds a woman of Paul Newman. He knows that she is not seeing him but something beyond. (This phenomenon is not just linked with stars.) If the perceiver doesn't realize it, the unrealistic perception is sure to ruin the relationship.

Our fantasies mature along with us and show us what we need. At different points in his life a man might fantasize about Jackie Onassis or Leontyne Price, depending on what image of the feminine completes his character. A woman might emulate Chris Evert at one age if she wants to be a tennis star and Marlon Brando if she needs to complement too much intellectualism with a more earthy physicality. How many blacks have not been inspired and sustained through difficult times by the example of Martin Luther King?

Writing in the *New York Times*, William Grimes describes the way his early adolescence was devoted to James Bond and the cult of 007. "Bond held forth the promise—intoxicating to a skinny, awkward kid with glasses—that brains as well as brawn could work for you in the wider world. . . . I still tend to approach all sorts of challenges as Bond."[1] But as he matured, the Bond model didn't hold up for him. "The 007 approach rests on the notion that every encounter is a struggle from which only two kinds of people emerge: a winner and a loser. . . . In this stark world view, knowledge becomes simply one more instrument of domination." He realized that Bond's taste in food ran to huge slabs of steak, that he knew nothing about literature, music, or art. "The superspy . . . was no longer up to the job." It was time for something new to come in.

Our dreaming and fantasizing about stars illuminate our desires for fame and fortune. The "stars in our eyes" show what excites us. Perhaps it is in the world of art or music or sport or politics. Our fantasized subjects can lure us on to greater accomplishment. A person may feel extremely low and have a dream about a famous person. The meaning of it may appear to be an impossible wish. But, if one persists in following the desire, he or she makes real progress toward the goal.

The star thinly veils a beckoning Inner Lover. If we can allow our imagination to play with the fantasies aroused by stars and identify what styles and aspirations they represent for us, we can use these stars as Inner Lovers to help us achieve what we want to do in the world.

PART THREE

The Many Lovers

Psyche and Eros

Around age fourteen I read Freud's *Interpretation of Dreams* and was rapt at the meaning he found in dreams. Later, in Jung's books I read about archetypal symbols, history, and the elements of fairy tales that were imbedded in people's psyches. Traditional mythical motifs—mothers, fathers, the child, heroic quests, initiations, cycles of death and rebirth, goddesses and gods, sacred spaces, sacrifice and transformation, demons, sun and moon, snakes, trees, roses, and inner gardens—abound in our psyches. Not only are they portrayed in the art, science, and anthropology of other cultures, but in our own life stories as well.

The Greek myth about Psyche and Eros serves well as a model for the soul bond—the Inner Lover dynamic—that I am explicating in this book. While the myth on the surface is about a man and a woman and perhaps tempts the reader to think of it as an ancient story about a couple, it is rather to be understood as the couple within us. Psyche is the soul, and Eros is love's desire. The drama of their separation clarifies the struggles we have with intimacy within ourselves and with others. When they are united, they produce joy, illumination, and a child. It is important to bear in mind as I summarize the story that it does not happen out there somewhere, but in the mind of every man and woman, whether they recognize it or not. Knowing the myth can help us find our way and perhaps be more accepting of the risks and tasks that intimacy requires of us.

The story starts off with a King and Queen who have three daughters. The older sisters have married in the conventional way. The youngest daughter, Psyche, is very lovely but has found no husband. The oracle—which represents our intuitive wisdom—announces that Psyche must be carried to a mountaintop and left there. Everyone is certain she will die. Psyche goes willingly enough, surrendering to her fate. What she doesn't know is that the god Eros has fallen in love with her, and yet, because he is a god and she just a mortal, he has to find a secret way of being with her.

Once Psyche is left alone on the peak, Eros has her carried to his hidden castle, where there is an abundance of treasures. She is asked not to contact her family or anyone else. She is told that Eros will come to her as a lover at night but that she will not be able to see him. In this way they pass many blissful nights together. At this point Eros is very much like an unconscious fantasy lover. They make love in the dark. Psyche becomes pregnant.

Eros is the son of Aphrodite and Zeus. Up to this time the gods and goddesses played with mortals at their convenience. Passions were ignited and destroyed. Psyche as a human has none of their powers. She represents a new dimension of soul commitment stirring in human consciousness, which begins when Eros falls in love with her. At this point both Psyche and Eros are undeveloped. He is still tied to Aphrodite. Psyche's new dimension of beauty is still unproven. Psyche's becoming pregnant, though, is an outcome of her taking the initiative to leave home on her own and not follow the conventional fate of her sisters. It represents development in that she had the guts to submit to a larger fate. What felt like submission to death turns out to be to a private nighttime commingling.

Psyche, however, starts feeling imprisoned and cut off from the rest of the world. She doesn't like staying in the dark. Her sisters, who embody conventional ego doubts, concern her, and she arranges to see them. They are envious of the wealth in her house and suggest to her that her lover may be a monster. Doubt and fear in the ego will view dark instinctual Eros as a beast. They urge Psyche to break her promise to him and look at him in the light. Psyche decides to risk doing so. At this moment she is going against divine order and rule. She, a lowly mortal, is rebelling against their authority, out of her need to know.

One night she takes an oil lamp to bed. (Oil is an elixir of the earth. Light comes from the union of fire and this earthly essence.) After she and Eros make love and he has fallen asleep, she dares to light the lamp. Seeing him strikes her with more passion for him than before. He looks magnificent—after all, he is the young god of Love. In her ardor Psyche allows the lamp to drop oil onto his shoulder. Eros wakes up in pain and, seeing that she has broken her promise to him, flees. Feeling betrayed, he goes back to Aphrodite's house and nurses his wounds.

This part of the story represents running away from love at signs of pain or lack of trust. Eros' retreat to his mother represents how we regress to a safe place (as in returning to "mother" or "the womb"), when we feel (temporarily) overwhelmed by outrage. Part of us wants to escape and not respond in the relationship. In this case, Eros' shock that Psyche could disobey him needs to heal.

The story also shows us that Eros cannot be known in full until more trials of consciousness are met. At this point Psyche takes over and does the necessary work that will eventually enable Eros to reveal himself. But neither of them knows that yet. Aphrodite, angry at the injury done to her son, tries to drive Psyche away with impossible tasks. While it seems that Aphrodite is persecuting Psyche, in a sense she is giving Psyche opportunities to develop her mettle.

Psyche meanwhile is ready to commit suicide as a result of having lost her lover. Prior to her daring act, Psyche really did not realize how much she loved him. She implores other gods and goddesses to help her, but they refuse because of their loyalty to the pantheon. Pan is the only one who helps her. He tells her to seek Eros with prayer and tender submission. She angrily kills off her sisters, which for her is a giant step forward in confronting the situation. She is no longer hampered by doubts. Thus, she goes to Aphrodite willing to do the tasks.

The first task is to sort out a huge jumble of seeds—corn, barley, millet, and so on—which Aphrodite has mixed together. She tries to turn Psyche into nothing more than a drudge. Psyche despairs at ever being able to finish this job. Surprisingly, ants come to do it for her. The implication is that in her unconscious she finds the aid she needs to communicate and order, sift, select, and evaluate. Sorting things out is a step that needs to be taken in the coming together of Psyche and Eros.

The second task is to gather the Golden Fleece of ferocious rams. This act would be like stealing the war power of the Pentagon or the Kremlin. Again, Psyche despairs at being able to do it. But she is instructed by the reeds of the river that after the rams come to drink, wisps of their wool can be gotten from the bushes nearby. In this way, Psyche learns from supple, flowing water plants about the indirect approach, as opposed to head-on confrontation, which would certainly fail. She also learns about waiting for things to change and taking a little bit at a time.

Psyche's ability to succeed at these tasks, despite her hopelessness, is determined by her love, which is Eros. He supports her although he is distant from her (like the invisible thread of connection lovers have). Aphrodite is furious. She assigns an even more difficult task, which is to obtain a flask of water from the River Styx. Guarded by dragons, the water seems totally inaccessible to Psyche. This time the eagle—the symbol of unconscious wisdom and courage—does it for her. It's important to remember that when we struggle hard, we dig deep and can unearth helpful eagle powers.

We can perceive several messages so far. Psyche has grown stronger and wiser by taking on the tasks. Psyche cannot do the tasks on her own—with her rational mind. She attracts divine helpers, which implies that such help is not only available but perhaps ordained.

The fourth task (in many spiritual traditions four is a symbol of wholeness) is the worst of all. In the first three tasks Psyche has integrated aspects of masculine power, such as the ram and the eagle. But now she must face essential feminine powers. She is to go into the Underworld and get Persephone's beauty secret. Her biggest challenge along the way is to avoid the temptation to pity other creatures. She must keep her eyes focused on the goal without looking left or right. She must not yield to her usual inclination to be compassionate or the temptation to be more beautiful, or, even more seriously, the desire to die.

Throughout the story Psyche has been despairing and suicidal at every point. In the Underworld (representing the unconscious), she can regress and stay there. How often do we get trapped in the vortex of being convinced that we can never make it no matter how hard we try or wish or visualize what we want? How often when all our efforts seem hopeless, are we stricken with loss and want to end the pain? In carrying out this task, Psyche manages to overcome the obstacles to reaching Persephone and getting the beauty box. But she seems to fail, for she opens the box just as she gets out of the Underworld. Persephone's beauty secret puts her in a trancelike sleep, like the one Sleeping Beauty and Snow White succumbed to, in which all life is held in abeyance.

Eros meanwhile has healed from his wounding and is so moved by Psyche's willingness to die for him and her superiority in love despite defeat that he rushes to rescue her from this sleep. Some interpreters believe he always sought Psyche but had not been able to act until then. He joins her in marriage and has it recognized as divine. The child born to them is Voluptas, meaning joy, bliss, or pleasure. The child is both human and divine.

Erich Neumann writes, "When Psyche is received into Olympus as the wife of Eros, an epoch-making development of the feminine and of all humanity is manifested in myth. Seen from the feminine standpoint, this signifies that the soul's individual ability to love is divine, and that transformation by love is a mystery that deifies."[1]

Despite Psyche's wounding of Eros, she always acted to preserve their bond. After killing off the old way of their being together, she tries to find a new way. She stands for the onset of relationship as part of the individuation process rather than just for sex and procreation. She becomes Eros' equal because she taught him that love was not just a sensual game in the dark but involved devotion and the sacrifice of illusions. She is heroic, often fighting against his resistance and withdrawal. Her perseverance brings about the inner marriage, which gives birth to joy. She brings a new dimension of beauty than heretofore represented by Aphrodite and sexual attraction. Psyche's beauty is the revelation of soul that love stirs. The bonding of Psyche to Eros involves discoveries of truths within oneself

The marriage of Psyche and Eros represents the culmination of the transformation of both of them. Their flux of trials of initiation and their ultimate union is reflected again and again on our love journeys. More than once we will find ourselves exposed on a cliff, anticipating a monster or death, and have to face tasks and be rescued by Eros.

In being penetrated by the desire of love, Psyche teaches us not to stay in the dark, and that in the act of sorting things out consciously, aid is available from powers in the unconscious. We learn to wait for the situation to change and to persevere despite frequent attacks of despair. We are to keep our focus on union and not get distracted by pity or fear.

This myth is indeed a majestic and numinous model for men and women as they experience the highs and lows of love. It addresses the malaise of separation people feel today by showing the need of the soul for love and the need of Eros for Psyche. Every time we struggle with love, we are caught at some place in the drama of Psyche and Eros. Our Inner Lover stories are our individualized versions of this model.

In *The Myth of Analysis*, James Hillman makes some other points about this evocative model. One is that the solitary hero myth is outmoded. As he puts it, "The opus of the soul needs intimate connection, not only to individuate but simply to live."[2] It is possible that our love situations and the intense emotions flowing out of them have more to do with the working out of our fate than anything else. They are mysterious as well because there is something more than a personal dimension to them.

We set off on a soul journey when we are engaged by another person. It is as if our soul awakes from a passive, asleep state, like Psyche's. This journey challenges the creative in us, ultimately tests and limits its potential.

The time before Eros and Psyche finally unite represents the importance of allowing space for suffering and imagination and growth. There need to be interludes to notice fantasies, body feelings, moods, and flights. In this context fear is helpful in that it creates time and distance to go slowly and carefully. Rejection, impotence, and frigidity are also part of Eros' way of delaying as order is brought out of the chaos of jealousies, losses, confusions, and turmoil. These are the times when the tasks of Psyche need to be worked on.

The interplay of Eros and Psyche—trusting and doubting, yielding and denying, opening and closing—is the way we come to know our authentic truths. When you are uncertain about your soul, you are not yet a vessel that can adequately contain the creative force of Eros.

The soul learns from the sudden shifts, frustrations, and deceptions of the erotic impulse; it can be wholly engaged and then gone; it has hatred and cruelties. It widens in complexity. It destroys one's false self in order to birth a truer self.

Thus, it is important to immerse yourself in projection and not willfully withdraw it. Do whatever one can to further the relationship with the loved one. Let the projection reveal its message and fall away of its own accord.

Love includes all the desires toward being with another, the hopes that the other finds his or her wings, the yearnings and need for love in return, and the many things that are embarrassing to admit to oneself or another. It can often seem safer to reflect alone than to confront another. But it is important to realize that "Love's goal is not know thyself, but reveal thyself." Be transparent, one who is seen and seen through, with nothing to hide. Be self-accepting. A soul that is loved is wholly revealed and wholly existential.

The story of Psyche and Eros is worth returning to again and again, for one finds oneself entering into it at different points in the cycles of relationship. It is especially helpful to remember how Psyche did not give up, even though she was despairing, and that aid does come from deeper sources than we know.

Indeed, the relationship between Psyche and Eros now is the equivalent of the heroic quest for the precious Grail in our time and culture. Thus, within the context of the Psyche-Eros drama, I want to take a closer look at a variety of relationships that test our souls and determine our destinies. These will include a long-term bond, such as marriage; a short affair; transference in the therapeutic situation; and a relationship that had its beginnings in early years and was later reactivated. I will also show that every relationship has a third player in it; that even when the outcome of love seems impossible, one can be empowered; that Inner Lovers are wonderful muses; that people of the same sex can be Inner Lovers; that the passion of Inner Lovers is of great import to the self one brings into the world.

These next chapters constitute what I have come to understand about the transpersonal aspects of love—how the down-to-earth fun and excitement, grief and anger, are tempered into a strong creative will. My fervent hope is to enable readers to try this message out for themselves.

Long-Lasting Bonds

In a long relationship, such as a marriage, there J will be greater peace if the boundaries between identities are observed, despite the tendency to blur the edges. To some extent our inner images of each other will add fire to the outer bond, but one is doomed to conflict if one doesn't make the effort to understand one's projections and the distinction between a lover and an Inner Lover.

I met the man I would marry when I was at Smith College. At this stage I knew nothing about the Inner Lover, but I did realize that my passion for writing surged, partly encouraged by my relationship with him. From the start I projected the image of great writer onto him more than myself. Like many women, I deprived myself by giving more attention to the man's creativity than my own. It would have been better to be excited about my own aspirations and the Brian-who-struggled rather than Brian-the-great-writer. But the paradox is that I would not have developed if I had not perceived and loved the heroic writer in him. As I see it now, it would be more accurate to say that I loved the images of passion and excitement that were aroused.

In a long-term relationship, while the other person is important to fuel one's fire, the distinction must be made between the image of the person within oneself and the outer person. Like

Psyche, one must light the lamp and risk coming out of the dark. Instead of just reveling in our one-sided thoughts and sensations about lovers, we must look at who they really are. (Also, as with Psyche, doing this inspires even more love.) In my case, the qualities that attracted me to Brian as a writer were qualities I wanted to increase in myself. Even though writing was a mutual obsession, I later was able to distinguish how separate our responses were to it. And, over time, as our original hopes did not materialize, we would use writing in different ways.

At college I immersed myself mostly in literature and writing courses. In my junior year I avidly read a local literary magazine and was particularly struck by Brian's stories. One sucked me into its vortex of rage, leaving me trembling with admiration. I already saw him as the next Norman Mailer and since he was Irish, James Joyce too. How could I meet him?

I devised a plan that provided me with an excuse to call him. I said that I was doing an article for the school paper about James Joyce and wondered if he would let me interview him. Sure he would.

With heart pounding—not only because I was about to meet a fantasy figure but also because of my trickery—I arrived at his fraternity house one Saturday morning at the appointed hour. (The "fraternity" he had chosen consisted of independents, who did not subscribe to the more traditional clubs; this radicalism made him more appealing.) I waited in a disheveled living room that had a beery scent. Down the wide carpeted staircase came Brian in a white t-shirt and jeans. He had a wide head with tousled black hair and large black eyes. (Later I would find out that he was just getting up after a heavy night of drinking, during which he had thrown some furniture out the second-story window, to everyone's amusement.) Sitting down with him, I nervously blurted out my prepared questions. He answered briefly. (Probably with a hangover he couldn't think very well.) I got out of there as quickly as possible.

I walked across the street to the cafeteria to recover from my escapade. He entered. When he saw me, he came over and sat down at the plastic-veneered table. I relaxed, now that the dupe was over. He made some jokes. His bare arms seemed especially attractive and vulnerable. I was in awe that I actually was talking casually with the writer whose stories I'd found so exceptional.

In the following weeks I anxiously wondered if I'd see him again. Then one day he called and asked me for a real date. During one of our first times together he jokingly threw a handful of dollars out the window. I was taken aback. This moment bespoke our differences.

He had one of the rare single rooms in his house, which was a cozy place to be with its soft couch, table with typewriter, and books of fiction. One evening he enchanted me by playing on a comment I made about the seasons. He grabbed my shoulders and said, "You're my season," kissing me happily. We would be together for two decades.

He wrote. I wrote. He sometimes gave me titles to stories. He could spin words wonderfully. He got special permission to write a thesis consisting of a collection of long stories rather than a literary paper. Giving full rein to verbal acrobatics and exploring his Irish Catholic background made this perhaps the most deeply satisfying period in his life. He was notorious on campus for his humor. (Sometimes it would seem he was given no room *not* to be funny.) Several of his friends were the most literary people I'd met in my short life (and would later make a mark in the world). We were madly in love and thought our match was made in heaven.

We began an argument about money in college that continued ever after in our relationship. In the beginning, I didn't see how we could marry on nothing. After college, I went to live with my father, carrying with me my longstanding determination to be loyal to him. In retrospect, I see that while consciously I thought there were obstacles to Brian's and my future, Fate, that weaver of destiny in the unconscious, took over and catapulted us into marriage, despite ourselves.

It happened this way. That autumn Brian came to visit me in Chicago. While my father played golf, Brian and I happily made love. Because at the time I was at the very end of my menstrual period, I told Brian that he didn't need to wear a condom. A few weeks later I was shocked to miss my next period. The numerous books I anxiously consulted said women cannot become pregnant except during ovulation. However, I learned that semen can live in the womb long enough for the onset of ovulation, and this is what had happened to me.

I never considered abortion. For one thing, at that time abortion was illegal. But most of all, once I actually realized I was pregnant, I glowed about this precious little embryo of ours growing inside me and instinctively protected it. By the end of that summer Brian knew he was going to have to serve in the army and had decided to enlist to be able to go to Europe. Basic training and intelligence school were next on the agenda for him that fall and winter. We could either get married or part ways. He wanted to get married. I agreed.

Things happened quickly. We married in the dismal atmosphere of Fort Dix, New Jersey, where he was going through basic training, with only my sister and his sergeant as witnesses. I had to leave for France before Brian because the airplane wouldn't carry me in the last months of pregnancy. Living in a hotel and wandering about Paris turned out to be a wonderful respite. Shortly after he joined me, I went into the hospital to have our daughter. We gave her a French name and took her home to a house in the bucolic environs of Verdun.

We had a two-story farmhouse, furnished with lace curtains, armoires, ornately carved beds, painted tiles, a television set, and no phone. On either side of the house were barns, in back an apple orchard. In this charming and yet very isolated setting I nurtured our baby for her first three years. I managed to write some stories and many letters but certainly my time for writing was curtailed. Brian spent weekdays at the army post.

A curious tension existed. While in college we had in common mutually enjoyable fantasies about writing and each other; now our lives were quite different. I felt ignored as he went off to work all day, and I had no one to talk to except my baby. When Brian announced that he was going to get up early in the mornings to write a novel, I experienced violent jealousy.

The demands of family and the routine of work continued when we returned to the United States, where Brian found a job as managing editor of a magazine. Obviously we were not two writers indulging in their art while the world paid them for it. I saw that Brian was not setting the world afire like Norman Mailer. It was hard enough for him to get a novel or some stories written, much less published. And I? I was getting even less written. The original fantasy that engendered our relationship had dissipated.

The problem for both of us was in not distinguishing between the Inner Lover and the outer one. We both had expectations of each other as spouse, parent of our children, and muse to one another that were not based on reality. Through pain and frustration I had to let go of the successful image I had of Brian as a writer and become the writer I wanted to be by myself. In my imagination he could still feed my writing desire and spontaneity, but I also had to see him as a separate person with his own problems. His jobs, his commitment to his own writing, the need to pay bills, being a father all vied for his attention too.

Our lack of understanding contrasexual dynamics or the interior "family romance" provoked trouble over the next fifteen years. Our very closeness had so enmeshed our images that we had not distinguished very well between "I" and "we." I often felt that the threads of my life were inextricably woven into his. This cloth would have to be forcibly torn apart, and it was not easy.

We were married from ages twenty-two to forty; we were young and ignorant about relationships, despite having many wonderful things going for us, namely two children, fidelity, and a home. When I became active in the women's movement, Brian was receptive to it and my new feminist friends. (They in turn liked him and envied our marriage.) When Brian was about thirty, he wanted to quit his editing job and write books on a free-lance basis. That summer we hired an Oxford University student as a part-time sitter for our children; he was a long-haired anarchist. As sexual energy flashed between him and me, Brian felt great jealousy, particularly of the student's freedom and independence. This experience was the catalyst he needed to strike out on his own. He was successful but often desperately nervous about the amount of work he had to do, as well as paying bills on an irregular income.

Our lack of awareness about handling conflicts destroyed hopes for peace. We hurt each other in repetitive angry scenes. Over the years parenting and sex were often sources of friction rather than harmony. I put the responsibility for the children first and constantly attended to their needs. Brian preferred being more casual with them. I was often critical of his not being like my father. We had insecurities held over from the past, which had not been made conscious. I was very unsure of being loved or appreciated. He wanted to be a star in my eyes. If I didn't laugh at a joke or disparaged an idea of his, he was hurt. I accused him of not "talking" to me but was also inarticulate myself. Drinking escalated, especially for him, and created more confusion. It got so we did not enjoy doing things together and for years did not go on a vacation.

As a couple we became like a walnut that looked fine on the outside but was all dried up inside. The warmth of Eros was extinguished between us, because we did not know how to access the inner helpers as Psyche did. Often when relationships end, there is a phase of sourness and stagnation, longer if the ego is unwilling to let change happen. I believe now that our relationship was supposed to end in order for us to have other life experiences but at the time I desperately resisted divorce. Divorce had been so painful to me as a child I'd vowed never to inflict it on my children. (I have a number of times had to submit to life's being more powerful than my vows!)

Seven years prior to what would be the official end, I had a strong meditative experience as I was working in my journal. I'd been focusing on an image that had come to me of a single rose turning in the dark. I used it as a mantra, repeating to myself, "Rose unfolding in the dark." I was suddenly surprised by an inner voice that stated very clearly, "You are going to have to leave Brian." This came from such a profound place that I was shaken. Did it really mean that I was to leave the marriage or just create more space between us? I agonized and chose to believe the latter while it was the former that was to be the truth. But at the time I was too afraid to face the end. Instead I tried to do everything to prevent it from happening, clinging to the barest shreds of love.

I began to wonder how much of the torrent of life I was holding back out of fear. The natural impulse of the ego seems to be to recoil or resist or try to control. What if I surrendered to the tide? I knew that I could be deceived by strong inner promptings. Since then I've discovered that if the urgings are repeated, they are signaling one's proper direction.

In an attempt to get a better perspective on our problems, I persuaded Brian to go to a marriage counselor with me. I'd recently learned of a Jungian analyst in town, a breed I thought would understand me. When Brian and I first started seeing him together, the experience of actually being with someone in a small quiet room and describing our life was totally strange and fearsome to both of us. Alan was tall and dark, with alert eyes and a cerebral calm that was very different from Brian's disorderly unrestrained manner. Alan's sense of being on top of his life seemed a welcome relief to the confused tangle of our affairs. In our first visit we talked about our desires as writers, my feelings of rejection, and Brian's feeling bad as a father and wage-earner. After the first session Brian was skittish and volatile.

A year and a half went by as Alan attempted to get us to discuss problems in supportive ways that did not escalate into the usual attacks. Brian throughout remained suspicious and resistant, and eventually wanted to quit.

I continued with Alan for therapy on my own, still looking for a way to improve things. Alan encouraged me to develop my life in other ways, so that I could appreciate more what I had with Brian. While my becoming more detached from Brian was supposed to lighten the tension, Brian became revengeful, seeing Alan as a rival. One day Brian said, "We have to kill this monster"—our marriage—"before it kills us."

The end was very hard. I got pneumonia, symbolically "being unable to breathe." Brian vacillated between warm nostalgia and angry abuse. His way was to try to block me out of his mind and have as little contact with me as possible. I went into silent, fearful mourning. I buried my wedding ring in my garden with the hope that I would have a new springtime in love. Divorce negotiations lasted a year. At the time we were officially divorced, Brian had married again. For several years I had problems with him over his payment of child support and alimony, involving two more court appearances. I felt enormous rage and helplessness, even while entertaining thoughts about being together. Detaching, letting go, and forgiving have taken years.

The following excerpt from my journal wasn't written until eight years after our parting:

> Can I at last say goodbye to the total way you were immersed in me or I in you? I want to see the world. I want to create. I want to live fully. I don't want that anchor around my neck/waist/feet. Oh, I so rarely had any freedom! . . . It was all too much for me. I loved you even though I was fighting you. It was an eternal conflict in my mind. But now I want peace and freedom. I am worth preserving. So goodbye, Brian. I kiss you, embrace you, and cut the cords with sharp teeth and hard eyes. I can at last say I look forward to my future. It too is hard. It is different. You are half the colors of my life. You are permanently there but I'm building new layers now.

After our physical parting I had dreamed of my horse being covered with mange from much neglect and starvation. Again and again I had to be reminded how I'd deprived myself, letting rats of indignation eat away at my good grain. There was much I had yet to learn. Not least of all was the need to affirm myself and not try to live through another. It would take other people and Inner Lovers to teach me how.

While our marriage ended, Brian as an Inner Lover figure still continued in my psyche. But now the way I see him in images and dreams reveals changes in my attitude to myself. Sometimes he has appeared as the engaging man of wit and words. Other times I am shown how he played on my pity for attention the way my mother did. Recently in a dream he died of congestive heart failure. I interpreted that as a vivid statement about his failings in matters of the heart. His dying in me would also mean that my failings of the heart would die away, enabling me, by implication, to have more capacity for intimacy toward myself and others.

Another woman told me of having a dream about her husband twenty years after their parting. Although he had abandoned her and their children, she had been working on forgiveness as time went by. In the dream she and he delicately embraced and separated, after which she felt the forgiveness had been accomplished.

Inner Lovers show us attitudes we have toward ourselves. We want to get them to be loving and supportive, but images and dreams don't lie. They can be counted on to show us where we are mean or cruel or vain or self-pitying, as well as where we are beautiful, great, and kind.

A thirty-five-year-old woman's sequence of dreams and commentary illustrates these points. In the first, she said, *My husband has an obvious feeling of success and refinement about him. He is standing side by side with another woman with dark, short hair, who is very focused, devoted, energetic, and ambitious. I think she belongs to him and is the major focus behind his success.* She reported that the dream brought up her feelings of inferiority in her position being usurped by another woman more than anything else. She had a long-standing problem of feeling inferior in many ways.

In the second dream, *My husband is angry about something and having a temper tantrum. He sweeps things off the table. I get angry and try to stop him but can't. Then afterwards he wants love and hugs but I won't do it because I am angry and don't feel like being understanding.* Here her dream shows not only her anger more blatantly than she was feeling in her outer life, but also the way she felt her husband was treating her.

While this woman, whose marriage was in its eleventh year, had many dreams about her husband, she also had an Arab man make an appearance in her dreams. In an early one he was going to take her to find some coins at the bottom of a polluted pool and she couldn't decide whether to have sex with him or not. (That is about the initial issue of trust.) He was to become a recurring and guiding Inner Lover, who helped her not be so dominated by her husband.

Long-term relationships get weeds, just like gardens. The most tenacious is the confusion of the inner love drama with the exterior problems of living together. Anne Truitt, a sculptor, writes in *Turn* that as a child, she'd fashioned a romantic hero for herself and discounted the boys around her. She cherished her image and projected it onto the man she married. "He shone for me as pure gold."[1] The radiance hid darker aspects of their marriage, and she clung to it through the marriage, their separation, his remarriage and death. She "could never pull off [this romantic ray] by will, reason, desperation, or prayer."[2] In her case she saw only the Inner Lover and not enough of the real person.

Usually disappointment and misfortune give one the opportunities to more clearly see the distinction between the image one carries and the actual person. In the following example, two people were able to struggle with harsh realities and maintain the strength of their inner images of each other.

This couple told me how their initial attraction to one another was based on a conversation they had about unconditional love being true love. They were equally committed to this ideal. They had met in the U.S. but the woman had to go back to her home in Israel. Their separation led to passionate calls and letters. The first sorrow for the woman came in deciding to leave her home to come to live with the man among strangers in Montana.

Soon after their marriage they lost their first baby. The man had a brief affair with another woman. The wife miscarried two more babies. She thought seriously of killing herself. The couple grew distant. The man escaped through drugs and sometimes saw another woman, soon after which the wife moved out. While she was away, she decided she wanted to try to rebuild what they'd had. Her husband received some counseling and got off drugs. They moved to a new city and started anew.

Here is what the husband had to say about their history: "Right from the first I had a deep knowing that I was not mistaken about her. I believed things were perfect the way they were though they were incredibly painful. The trouble we had was part of a process I wouldn't want to do without. On a deep level I wasn't worried about our relationship, although on the surface it seemed like I wanted her to leave. I always thought she would come back. In the beginning when we had said that true love is unconditional, then we would say to ourselves, hey, this is a person who's going to deal with my shit, and that's wonderful. I think we decided we would really allow the other person to be who they were and through that heal each other. I think that's what we're doing."

She adds, "Now we don't have the passionate love we had when we first met, but it is so much deeper. It feels endless. The bond we have is beyond anything, as if nothing at all can hurt it. We also got back our playfulness and got over our heaviness."

Their initial idealism received severe shocks. In coping with devastation, they still kept strong inner and outer ties. (They finally had a child, too.)

A searing problem in long-term relationships is handling passionate attractions to other people. In the United States, more than in Europe, it's generally assumed that if one is attracted to another, that means one no longer loves one's partner, and both agonize over whether or not to leave the partner. Many people suffer enormous guilt over this unnecessarily. One in this situation may ultimately decide to leave, but at first it may be wiser to explore the passion *inside oneself* and see where it wants to go— that is, how it might contribute to one's own character development or enrich one's life. Knowledge of the Inner Lover concept gives us more power to choose whether to pursue an outer relationship or concentrate on the inner.

Equally important is not to try to deny or suppress the attraction. As Garrison Keillor wrote, "Passionate love . . . has the power to arouse us from the couch, whip us into shape, light the bonfire of curiosity and propel us on lifelong adventures against staggering odds."[3] We don't need to miss that energy. The problem is how to handle such power.

I know a woman who had several such attractions, all the while staying with her outer partner. It was always difficult, but that is the crux of passionate love no matter what one's outer situation is. The woman was able to let the images generated by the attractions feed her as Inner Lovers. One of them was a man who was very much a sophisticated New Yorker. As a result of working with this man imaginally, she initiated a move to New York City, where her creativity flourished. Then she met an artist who did his work all over the world. This impelled her to become more adventurous in her life. In both cases she had contact with these men but not enough to break up her primary bond; she was able to let the energy transform her.

It takes knowledge and awareness to be able to separate the images of the Inner Lover from the outer one, and to appreciate the distinctions between them. It's like being an acrobat riding two horses that are moving in tandem, either of which might break away at any moment.

But when we can fuel our lives with Inner Lovers, we and those around us will be much more fulfilled. Our world expands and possibilities are freed up for both partners.

Love's Eternal Triangle

When we talk about love, we rarely speak of triangles. The assumption is generally made that triangles are when three people are involved with each other. The "other" woman or man does loom large on many an erotic landscape. Perhaps the basis for the imprint of the triangle comes from infancy when we were part of the original triangle of our self, our mother, and our father. At first we thought we were all one. Then we discovered that we and our mothers and fathers were different, like points on a triangle, albeit connected.

Ethel Person says that everyone will hit upon the triangle experience, and that it will be important in one's history, whether enriching or depleting. It happens whether we are part of a monogamous couple or not. How we handle it will be indicative of the quality, wisdom, and decorum of things inside us.

The third party to a relationship is not necessarily another person. It could be the partner's work or travel, or whatever is perceived as "the problem" when we try to make the relationship turn out the way we want it to. It is the part that neither partner can control or possess; it is the very will of the relationship itself.

Draw close to this mysterious player. Inner Lovers know it well. Before going into Inner Lover dynamics any further, we must take a closer look at this important aspect of relationship.

In my marriage, for instance, much as I wanted to keep love alive, nothing would have made it last forever. It seems that destiny required the relationship to change form. I believe my marriage ended because it had served its purpose and it was important for me (and Brian) to be enlarged by other challenges. We tend to forget that love is not just personal. A more universal Self works through us without much consideration for our ego's needs.

Near the end of my marriage, intuitively sensing the presence of a "third party," I wrote:

> They are married but there is a third person, invisible but palpable, who lives with them. From time to time they've wondered who It could be but they've never been able to figure it out.
>
> When they first met, they were so close, they didn't see It. Then came the babies and the bills. . . . Suddenly one day they both noticed the third presence living with them and It was not unlike another child. It was annoying, demanding, and imperious. When they fought, It appeared when they tried to leave each other.
>
> It sometimes took the form of a monkey laughing at them or a snake doing an erotic dance or a spider weaving visions. They couldn't figure out why It wouldn't leave.
>
> Then they decided to ignore It. . . . Left alone, it began to rearrange the home the way It wanted it. It made the place light and airy and brought in people for parties. It celebrated whenever It could. The man and woman decided to let It run the show, and they would come as guests.
>
> "That's the way it should be," It said.

The third player carries the destiny of a relationship. Relationships, like flowers, have seasons as well as life cycles with beginnings and endings. The cast of characters in our lives must change for our growth. As fire consumes wood, the flame of love burns until its object is burned to ashes, until there is nothing left to burn. It's possible that life may want us to know a variety of alliances, and humans out of fear have resisted and tried to perpetuate the ideal of the lifetime mate. As our lifespan has lengthened to well beyond the child-rearing stage, we have time for more psychological growth. The evolution of civilization hinges on our bringing forth our potentials, evoked so well by our attractions.

John R. Haule in *Divine Madness* writes about a "Third" factor in a relationship.[1] His thesis is that to stay close means to pay attention to all the feelings and images we have about the relationship, whether serious or playful. We stay close to the Third by defining our thoughts and awaiting clarification, without knowing what we are looking for. It is there regardless of our awareness. Its job is to balance everything.

We get off base when we can't endure the tension and tenderness that gives the Third its opportunity. We want an immediate solution and seek outside advice. Then our relationship trudges along in an ordinary way.[2] When guided by the Third, relationships sparkle. (The exercises that I provide at the end of this book on working with images and dreams and inner dialoguing help immensely in staying attuned to this third party.)

This player helps love do its creative work. If we resist the tendency to want to direct the relationship out of fear, this player will ignite more and greater love in one. It will light up dark places in one's interior self.

When we feel "in love," we become acutely aware of the boundary of our self in regard to the other. I am this known entity, me. You are a different entity. I want you. But we are acutely aware of the space between me and you, between my skin and your skin. It is the space of not having what we want. Into this space flow fantasies about the person. When our imaginations roam freely in dream and reverie, deep sources of meaning and creativity are activated in our psyches. To tend your imagination in this way is to feed your soul.

Thus, for all of us there is another eternal triangle, consisting of the I, the you, and the space between. Here is where the Inner Lover concept is most dynamic.

Anne Carson in *EROS the Bittersweet* writes of love being beautiful (in its object), foiled (in its attempt), endless (in time). All of us see the object of our desire as beautiful in some way. We reach out for it and in some way we get what we don't expect.

We think we are reaching for the other person, but we are reaching because we feel an incompletion in ourselves, a lack. The other person represents qualities of being we need to take into ourselves.

The Inner Lover appears to us in the imaginal space between us and the other person. We feel this space between as absence or lack that we arduously try to fill. The obstacle or third player defers, obstructs, makes one hungrier, intensifies desire. Images of Inner Lovers heal the wound in us created by the obstacle.

We may try to avoid the pain by various strategies. If instead we meditate on our Inner Lovers, we will experience the promise of Eros, which, perhaps more than the person, excites and satisfies us, as well as terrifies and awes us. We will be able to embrace all the feelings and embarrassments of our attachments and thereby reach new territories.

We will miss the grand adventure of Eros if we try to take detours. For instance, if someone is terrified by being shaken up or vulnerable, she or he might try to dominate the other person. In this way the other person will lose the freedom to grow and will be damaged. This happens when we are afraid we will lose someone or lose their admiration and therefore devise ways to imprison him or her.

Or a person may back away from emotional passion and only permit affectionate friendships. (This starves the soul.) Another route is to discard the beloved as soon as the period of fascination is over. Alternatively, some people can let their emotions so overwhelm them that they neglect to take care of themselves.

The stress and ambiguity of Eros or the third party needs to be lived with over time, in one situation after another, as both partners go through changes. Living with Eros, regardless of the frustration—space, illness, another person, or work—is a most fruitful and worthy enterprise. Keeping Eros alive will keep our soul alive. Anne Carson compares being aware of the third player to "watching a fire move along a rope that binds (the couple) together."[3] She writes, "Truly good and indeed divine things are alive and active outside you and should be let in to work their changes. . . . Erotic mania is a valuable thing. . . . It puts wings on your soul."[4]

We reach out toward a meaning in our loves that eludes us. "It is a reach that never quite arrives, bittersweet."[5] But if we do not follow our desire through to the end, our wings stay clipped. We will never see the new vistas.

It may seem difficult because at any moment we are caught in the midst of several triangles: mother-father-I, lover-I-Inner Lover, I-lover-obstacle/relationship itself/third player. Like Psyche, to join with Eros, we need to persevere and to realize that each relationship unfolds purposefully.

The Inner Lover in Therapy

The way erotic love behaves in therapy throws the Inner Lover concept into sharp relief. Although not everyone will have such a therapeutic experience, the experiences I discuss in this chapter illustrate in a very clear way another view of the role the Inner Lover plays in all of us.

I noted at the beginning of the book that I first became aware of the Inner Lover dynamic when I went through analysis—a process that forces one to carefully examine one's feelings and fantasies. Such an experience is valuable, and if navigated well by the therapist, it can be enormously so. It is a journey not only about one's relationship to oneself but also with the therapist, which can evoke many life-changing possibilities.

Freud was the first to characterize the feelings a subject had for the therapist as "transference" and the therapist's feelings for the client as "countertransference." The experiences that these psychological terms denote are also common in our everyday relationships outside of therapy. They include the bundle of feelings, both erotic and hostile, that we have about another person, especially in intimacy. Transference is akin to projection. The love attachment to the therapist opens up the subject's unconscious (and vice versa). The emotions of childhood—resentment, helplessness, fear, dependence, jealousy—are discussed, as if under a microscope. The transference in therapy is a powerful subject because it brings to the surface the many points at which the person is cut off from life or numbed. The relation between Psyche and Eros is evident.

Jung saw sexual desire as a psychological expression as well as a biological instinct. It is the pathway our souls use to get through to us. Erotic love for a therapist is not just a sublimated incestuous wish but has a great deal to do with an individual's coming to love his or her own soul, through the ability to accept and value its yearnings, however embarrassing and chaotic they may seem. This erotic love will spawn many creative acts as it burns.

Transference often occurs when erotic fantasy fills the gap between two people, especially in intimate settings where there is no physical contact. Countertransference, when the therapist has sexual fantasies about the client, is a sign, Jung thought, of not paying the right attention to the client, either over- or undervaluing him or her.[1] Ethel Person, who has written extensively about transference in therapy, says that it "remains both gold mine and mine field," depending on how it is handled.[2] It can make a therapist uncomfortable because he or she must not take the subject's feelings too personally or literally but more imaginally and in a way that is deeply related to the subject's psyche.

Person has observed that women are more susceptible to transference than men, because women tend to eroticize power and men like the safety of that lofty position. It is thus more likely to occur between male therapists and female clients than any other combination. Also, the less power one feels personally, the stronger the transference will feel.

The famous male analysts themselves have been notoriously susceptible to certain female clients. Toni Wolff, after she finished analysis with Jung, was openly acknowledged as his companion along with his wife; she became an important therapist herself but never married. Otto Rank became attracted to writer Anaïs Nin and for a while they worked together, until she determined she did not want to be a therapist.

For a therapist to cross the boundaries and indulge in actual sex with a client is considered unethical by the majority, but there are many who do not conform (as in the case of a psychiatrist who treated the poet Anne Sexton and whose affair with her was revealed in the biography *Anne Sexton* by Diane Wood Middlebrook). When sex takes place physically as opposed to imaginally, the necessary detachment for free discussion is thereby eliminated. The client, still bound and blind from the past, imitates old patterns. Instant gratification replaces the fruits of understanding.

When all the energies aroused in transference-countertransference are instead openly acknowledged, the "excessive and unrealistic demands and conflicts, which have been destructive to real-life relationships, can be brought to the fore," according to Ethel Person. Self-knowledge helps free the subject from endless cycles of repetitive compulsion in order to enjoy the creative or restorative aspects of love. Obviously, actual indulgence in sex would cast a dark entangling net around the pair, blocking beneficial insights from coming to light. That is not to say that intimate talk is not filled with its own lacunae and blind spots as well. But even if a therapist-client relationship ultimately ends in betrayal or denunciation, it can be constructive for the individual who discovers that she has enough self-respect to leave the situation.

My experience with Alan fell somewhere between a gold mine and a minefield. As will be seen, I had to struggle to separate the fantasies I had of him from the way the relationship was going—a process that taught me much about the Inner Lover.

I described earlier how my husband, Brian, and I had gone to a Jungian marriage counselor, and I continued seeing him privately.

Picture me then, thirty-five years old, in this man's office for weekly visits. He always wore a suit and sat in a gold wingback chair. I sat on a leather couch to his right. A glass coffee table was in front of the couch. In back of him were bookshelves. He listened and responded to me. For years I'd been starved for such attention. I talked to him about my writing and psychological and spiritual interests, subjects I couldn't talk about with Brian. This talk was very pleasurable to me. It was probably my greatest need. Significantly, I asked him about himself—as one does in conversation—and he responded. Another therapist might demur such questions and analyze why I needed to take the focus off myself. But he didn't. In fact, he seemed glad to talk about himself.

These excerpts from "Therapy's Tender Trap," an article in a women's magazine, describe some of the nuances of such a situation:

> After the initial "cure" from the outpouring of painful feelings and memories received positively by the therapist, other strivings and yearnings begin to emerge. Very quickly the patient feels that she should be given more. . . . This "more" can be experienced in a number of ways. She may want reciprocal intimacy: to have the psychiatrist tell her something about himself. She may want dependent gratification: to be taken care of. She may want teaching: to have a wise older person tell her how to live her life. She may want insight: to understand herself better. . . . She becomes then a supplicant, using the full panoply of psychological and interpersonal skills developed during childhood and early adult life, which, for women in our culture, means being compliant, pleasing, cute, beguiling, seductive, attractive and often ensnaring, to obtain gratification for these re-emergent yearnings.
>
> How does this middle-aged, sedentary, often bored and lonely man react? . . . The favorite patient, as study after study has shown, is a young, attractive, verbal, educated female. Such women obviously fill a void in many therapists' lives.
>
> So a mutual seduction is launched, and a strange kind of love affair ensues. Since the therapeutic transaction usually allows for considerable daydreaming on the part of the therapist, he is free to imagine whatever he wants as long as he keeps his eyes fixed on the patient. . . . Now, what is the harm in all this? One potential hazard, of course, is the participants will move beyond fantasy and develop a physical relationship as well. This is always destructive for the patient and disastrous for the psychiatrist as well.
>
> Mutual erotic attraction, then, increasingly becomes a reciprocal dependency for emotional gratification, and the problem of interminable therapy. Far better to expend that love in the outside world where, with all its dangers and ambiguities, a solid return is more likely. . . . The psychotherapist can be a useful transitional object, like a Teddy Bear; but he must be given up, or moved beyond, as soon as possible.[3]

At the beginning I had no such perspective. I was innocent and vulnerable, feeling dead and hard as bone, afraid of a sick marriage and a sick father.

About six months into the therapy one night I woke up suffused from head to toe with warm sun rays. I did not understand it then but it was the arousal of Inner Lover energy. I felt enormously attracted to Alan. It felt exactly like being in love.

In sessions week after week I had to express my longings for him. Having to speak one's feelings is certainly one of the most difficult challenges in therapy. Fears, shame, tears well up. But one dares to say what one feels, regardless of the other's not responding in kind, in order to value oneself I had to overcome the habit I had had since childhood to be mute and withdrawn about my own intensity, out of fear of rejection. Early on Alan said that the sexual feelings were mutual but he wanted to move very slowly. One time he came over and sat close to me on the couch. I wanted to put my hand on his leg but was too scared to. He said to me: "I want you to have a full psychological experience. . . . I think your creativity is being aroused and you are experiencing it as love for me. . . . You look very appealing."

Alan's remarks made an actual affair with him seem possible, which no doubt prolonged and intensified my desires. I had no idea that he would continue to hedge about the boundaries, without ever owning up to the reasons. He said our first step in broadening the relationship beyond the therapeutic would be to try doing some projects or workshops together. These meetings started an avalanche of tortuous desires that continuously went unfulfilled. I felt ashamed of my desires; therapy at this point was not helping me to value them even if they could not be realized. My having grown up as a child unaccepting of my innermost being was an old wound that deepened.

However, as the months went by, deeply numinous images appeared inwardly. In a dream, *I find Alan's penis on the ground, pick it up, and eat it. It seems like manna and radiates through my being.* In another dream, *We are having dinner. He is a god and I am a goddess.* These dreams led me to read myths about Dionysus and reaching the divine through sexual ecstasy. I was fascinated

84

by Par Lagerkvist's novel *The Sybil*, in which a young girl receives the deity (actually a goat) in a dirty, dank pit in the temple of Delphi. She incarnates both animal and divine potentialities. I was also inspired by Lou Andreas-Salomé, who had liaisons with Nietzsche, Rilke, and Freud, and wrote about the link between sexual excitement and creativity.

Because Alan had been a minister, I think my attraction to him concerned spiritual matters. I wanted to participate in his knowledge of Jung, myths, and God. When others suggested to me that Alan was a stand-in for my father, I asked him what he thought about that interpretation. He disagreed with this interpretation. He thought I wanted an equal partner. He rarely related my experiences back to my childhood, which I now believe he should have done.

During this time I was using exercises from Ira Progoff's Intensive Journal method to help me with the problems of my life. (See part five "How to Use Inner Lover Fantasies," for more description about these techniques.) The following excerpt from my journal illustrates how an inner dialogue facilitates exploration of an issue.

ALAN: We have to force-bloom what we have.

VALERIE: I can't face you. I want to dissolve.

ALAN: You want to annihilate yourself in me, when really you are strong and good.

VALERIE: But why can't we love each other?

ALAN: We can circumspectly. I am sad too. You are an exciting woman.

VALERIE: I want to sit in your lap and stroke your cheek.

ALAN: Love yourself first. Don't just love yourself if others do. You are a piece of divine light. You deserve to respect and honor the you in you.

VALERIE: Maybe you don't know just how wild and far-reaching I want to go.

ALAN: You need to go by yourself. I can't take you into dangerous ground. Take responsibility and don't look to me for approval.

VALERIE: I do thank you for making me feel sexy and strong. I guess we could nurture that.

ALAN: I'd like that. It's a fire we can both enjoy.

Such a dialogue helped make me more aware of behavior I needed to change. For instance, it stresses not submerging my identity in the man. It indicates I want to become wilder than ever and that if I do tend to myself and my own excitements, we would both enjoy the relationship more.

Once Alan said he liked my perfume. The remark led me to write about my "real scent" coming from my skin in moonlight and sunshine, my perspiration, my hair, my vagina. I was beginning to appreciate my essence in all its rankness more than ever.

I had a dream in which *I find on a shelf in my father's apartment many bottles of dried flowers*. In Alan's office as I made the connection between the dried-up flowers and passionate urges in my past, I grew faint. I realized how I'd repressed my sexual instincts all through high school and early college. As a result, I felt ugly and worthless. I could not let myself die in that way anymore.

I used the energy of my desire to write stories. In one I was a shaggy feral mare who is fucked by a black stallion with wild red eyes in dark, primeval mud. Then I was an ungroomed crone, a wise healer, witchy, close to nature. Or dancing in a red skirt and thin white blouse while flames licked my spine. I also wrote about Virginia Woolf, Sylvia Plath, and Dido (when she is left by Aeneas), women who turned their fury against themselves rather than their betrayers. While I wrote about women killing themselves or their children, at the same time I fantasized about lovemaking with Alan. I had yet to recognize my rage.

Then came a session during which he sat next to me and rubbed my belly and touched my breasts, whispering in my ear, "I want whatever you want in addition to the analytical hour." Subsequently he said that he was against our having more of a relationship, leaving me bewildered.

Just as women who are victims of rape or beatings often think something is wrong with them, so I tended to blame myself and was unable to confront him with my rage. I began to think he used his authority as a therapist to justify his own position, which made it very difficult for me to learn to trust my own voice or views.

As I began to see Alan as a wounded healer, I lost trust in him. At one point Brian went to see him privately to discuss his jealousy and it seemed obvious Alan was enjoying his power without taking any responsibility for his role in the jealousy. I felt betrayed and told Alan I would not continue to see him if he saw Brian. He didn't.

I kept pondering how this analytical relationship was similar to and different from one with a lover. Even while I lost respect for Alan personally, I still had intense longings. My breakthrough to him as an Inner Lover occurred when I experimented in my fantasies by calling Alan a different name. In this way I could relate to the inner Alan, who behaved differently from the outer one. The inner one was positive and helpful. I needed his support. Using a different name for him helped me deal with the outer relationship more realistically.

In a sardonic dream *Alan sneaks up behind me and kisses me. He offers me his penis. I put it in my mouth, and he ejaculates. I don't like his manner. He says gleefully, "That's what you wanted, isn't it?"* I did not want to be used coldly. Such a dream warned me about the outer Alan, as well as harsh attitudes I carried toward myself Yet every day I was filled with the enormous sun energy of Eros permeating my body, pushing, pushing, pushing, forcing a transformation of my psyche.

I consulted my friends. One said that if I broke the therapeutic bond, he'd have to choose to be with me or not. She said men who could not choose passion and potential over family and security did not really live. You either choose to follow psyche or perish. I was eager to break this news to him.

When I did, he said angrily, "You are trying to do with me what you can't do with Brian." Perhaps I *was* focusing on him because it was too painful to break with Brian. He persuaded me to stay on, and I said I would, as long as we were preparing to end. We didn't discuss the pain of abandonment that prompted my action nor the pain of leave-taking.

I realized how my inability to break with Alan was like the loyalty I had to my father and Brian. It was a loyalty that felt like a duty, depriving me of spontaneity and self-fulfillment.

I then betrayed my therapist with another by deciding to go see someone else about my relationship with him. I chose an older woman who had been Anaïs Nin's analyst. I thought that anyone who was so appreciated by Anaïs could help me. Hearing the situation, this woman made three salient points. One was that she compared Alan right away to my father—as distant, one whom I only saw at prescribed times, one from whom I sought expressions of affection. Another was to ask if I'd really like to break up his family. (No.) And, thirdly, she said that it had been very brave for me to come see her.

Around that time Janet Malcolm published an article on psychoanalysis in the *New Yorker* in which she said patients act out toward the analyst (for instance, by becoming defiant, conciliatory, or withdrawn) the way they felt toward parents, even if they don't remember the way they used to be. Remembering is the goal of all the impulses to act out. (I think I yearned to behave in the ways I never did: to have temper tantrums and get noticed.) She also said a patient may leave therapy because of unconsciously sensing what the therapist is caught in feeling (the countertransference). Both seek to know the real relationship between the two. And, finally, analysis ends when patients accept that the therapist will not satisfy their wishes and they must fulfill them in outer life.

I could see how like my father Alan was in his being distant and aloof. But although Alan had not had the courage to be responsible for his own behavior in our therapy, he had affirmed my femaleness and talked to me more intimately than either my father or husband had. My soul had been awakened, even if it had been in outrage against him. Some years afterward I had a dream in which *I am in a dentist chair, and he comes up behind me. I start to choke with a scream wanting to come out. He puts his arms around my chest, his fingers on my breast, and I yell at him not to touch me, that he had not helped me because he had no tears.*

Yet to leave him I had to face feelings of intense loss. I wondered how I could express the strong physical union I imagined with him other than sexually. In an inner-dialogue exercise he said, "You can be forceful in word and feeling. You can release it there. Just like in orgasms. Bring your animal and mind together. Don't keep them so far apart. Be in that sexual strength. It's power, vitality. It's yours. You are really trying to deny it instead of being it. Be as energetic as you feel. Don't be so polite." (It takes a long time to incorporate such a message. I have to come back to it again and again to really affirm it.)

A friend who is a therapist said I should leave him instantly because he wasn't "with me" as I worked out my feelings—he was against me. She said he should be so much more supportive of me.

Meanwhile I was separating from Brian and in pain and misery. My father was declining as well. The three major men of my life were all nearly gone from me. At this point I had a profound and surprising single encounter with Tom (described in a later chapter), which forced me even more to see the distinction between the lover in my fantasies and the actual person. It dramatically caused my Inner Lover image to shift from Alan to the figure inspired by Tom. I told Alan about the process, feeling this realization culminated our work together. He sounded relieved to be let off the hook.

Shortly afterward I ended therapy with Alan. He would have continued with me but I knew I could not get the support I needed as I descended more deeply into early childhood realms. I'd finally gotten the strength to oppose him. Yet in our last session I told Alan there would always be a special place in my heart for him and gave him a hug (ever-appeasing). He said he felt the same way and that we'd creatively traversed delicate waters. For me the parting scene was more obligatory than profoundly felt.

Through the unleashing of powerful erotic energies symbolized by the Inner Lover inspired by Alan, I was given a greater sense of my feminine worthiness and the will to go through with the risky travail of divorce. It was a beginning, but I had not faced the rage at being rejected or at having affection and his true feelings withheld. My keen disappointment at having been failed simmered beneath the surface as I left him behind and contemplated my next step. It's important to realize that an Inner Lover can take one just so far, before one needs another.

One of the basic lessons I learned, though, was to pay attention to what was produced by the impossibility of having him as a lover. In the next section I examine other kinds of situations in which the outer relationship is blocked but the inner one can flower beyond usual expectations.

Impossible or Inappropriate Lovers

When you are not able to live your love out with another person, all the energy turns back and excavates deeper layers in yourself. Jung had this to say:

> For the unconscious always tries to produce an impossible situation in order to force the individual to bring out his very best. Otherwise one stops short of one's best, one is not complete, one does not realize oneself. What is needed is an impossible situation where one has to renounce one's own will and one's own wit and do nothing but wait and trust to the impersonal power of growth and development.[1]

He suggested that the thing to do if you are up against a wall is to be still and put down roots like a tree, until clarity comes from deeper sources to see over that wall. The following scenario shows how difficult it can be waiting for deliverance when love seems impossible:

> She does not love him, she is unavailable, she is in some way wrong for him, and the man is left holding his love, her love, their love.
> All he has left is his body.

He is driving his car and all of a sudden has the sensation that she is in his arms and that he is pressing against her body, and he feels her familiar warm shoulders against his. and the familiar tilt of her head as he kisses her. And now he is longing to fuck her, to take her as deeply as he can. Then he is stepping into a fire and burning up.

At home he forces himself to make an omelet, to cut up vegetables tor a salad. Chopping a tomato, he slices off the tip of his thumb. The pain is sharp, like being pierced with barbed wire. The blood gushes and continues to gush under cold water. He tries a paper towel; the red seeps through. Then a handkerchief; it won't stop bleeding, just like his heart. He sits down in a chair and wishes he were dead.

In bed he dreams he is kissing her cheeks, then her lips. She is the warm, tender, wonderful woman whom he felt thrilled to just be around. Then they have their clothes off, and they are enclosed in a sexual embrace, and he is about to penetrate her when he wakes up, his body wet with perspiration.

This kind of thing happens again and again.

Pictures he has of her make him sullen, as though all he has of her is made of paper. He knows her smile all too well.

He just gets by in work. Things are forgotten. He hasn't the energy to put out much effort. He drinks too much coffee and gets a stomachache, and the scotch he drinks to get a little peace before going to bed only lasts a while.

He begins to feel as if he's gone into hiding in a cave to mourn her. He feels bereft, an ugly, worthless man, getting old to boot.

His body feels like a stone surrounded by burning sands. He himself is being consumed. He no longer has skin. Pretty soon there will be nothing left but ashes and smoke.

He is exhausted. Why the hell is he so affected by a goddamn woman anyway? Besides, she had qualities he didn't like.

Time passes. He has to go to work, buy groceries, do laundry, get gas for the car, etc. At times he becomes over-poweringly sad at the loss of his hopes. Deprivation seems the norm.

The change is already happening. More and more, rage sets in, like dark clouds that will not budge. His life seems empty without her. Even though she is not there, he feels imprisoned by her. But he can't get out of his cell.

One night he is in bed imagining her, with his eyes closed and his fingers arousing his penis. As waves of pleasure radiate outward, he is aware of an immense desire for life. Something outside him has taken over, commanding him to live. When finally the orgasm comes, his body relaxes at last.

When it appears that a desired relationship can't happen in the outer world—whether because the other person does not love us in return or some other reason—again and again we must recover the will to live. Our desire for the other sometimes feels so strong we demand the other to respond in kind. But there are some persons with whom actual relationships would be either too complicated or self-destructive, such as married people, certain business associates, students or teachers, doctors, or spiritual counselors. We all know relationships do develop between such persons, but usually that is because we don't know how to back off from them. We don't realize that we have the option to relate to them on an inner level only. In fact, these objects of longing and desire very often make powerful Inner Lovers. Knowing how to use them for our benefit when the outer flow is impossible or inappropriate opens up new creative avenues.

We deserve love, attention, and commitment from outer lovers. If we know that we have the ability to choose not to enter liaisons, through which these needs will not be met, we won't settle for less out of neediness and denial.

The media regularly reports "crimes of passion," which are demands carried to extremes. John Hinckley shooting Ronald Reagan because of Jodie Foster's inaccessibility and Jean Harris shooting Herman Tarnower for not loving her the way she wanted him to are two well-known examples. In both cases the energy was so strong that the person resorted to a violent act, which resulted in their being imprisoned, with their beloveds terrorized or dead. Josephine Hart's *Damage*, a recent best-seller, features a man who ends up killing his son because he cannot contain his instincts and let them work their changes.

The desperateness of these acts shows us how intensely desire and longing burn in us. Passion is in fact an element equal to water, fire, earth, or air. In Teilhard de Chardin's statement that if we could harness the energy of love, we could transform the world, the point is that passion can be used to contribute to our development as persons—it does not have to be damaging to others.

The problem is we feel that if we can't possess the person, we are cut off from love. We think we will not get any love. Nothing could be further from the truth, when we recognize the Inner Lover concept. How then does one refrain from a potentially destructive relationship and maintain contact with the Inner Lover?

First, it is important to recognize potentially difficult cases. Women are especially susceptible to teachers, doctors, counselors, and other authority figures who represent the power that some women severely lack in themselves. Women will attach themselves to a "great man" in a serving way. Picasso's wife, Jacqueline, took care of all his needs and, when he died, said she had nothing to live for. She saw no life of her own. Many, many women devote themselves to men of ideas, making up vast audiences for their lectures or programs, giving the men a great deal of warmth and money.

Men, on the other hand, often become very attracted to nurses, secretaries, or students, because they need the nurturing support and admiration that such women supply.

Offices these days have become the meeting ground for many people. One may be violently attracted to someone in the office with whom an actual relationship would be very compromising. Many of us are learning how to see a person every day and to maintain a balance between being businesslike and true to our feelings. It is not necessary to leave a job because of your attraction to a coworker as long as you can nurture the Inner Lover on the fantasy level.

A married teacher with children wrote about why she decided to have just a platonic friendship with a student, with whom there was a strong sexual attraction. She felt that the attraction was based on the excitement of learning. "The bond between teacher and learner has already opened the gate to the magic garden. *It doesn't get any better than this* [her italics]. Sexual relations are almost redundant, and they can destroy."

At the same time she managed to incorporate the creative excitement of such an attraction: "I taught better this spring than I ever have. . . . Like anyone with a crush, I tried to look terrific all the time, which meant being healthier and more animated. . . . If I could judge only by my spirits and performance, I'd pray for an attraction to resist every semester."[2]

In his practice Jung experienced a remarkable example of how the psyche could be trusted to reach a turning point on its own. A woman became convinced that she would marry him, even though he already had a wife. She set the date for the wedding. To all outer appearances she was completely off base, but she went ahead and acted according to her inner prompting. Just before the wedding date, her psyche instructed her not to go through with it, and she told Jung the wedding was off.

If we are feeling desperate and deprived, as a result of our attraction to an unavailable person, we can pamper ourselves as though needing intensive care. That means long baths, massage, good meals, rest, exercise, communion with nature, or anything else conducive to spiritual refreshment. We should avoid attempting to distract ourselves through overscheduling, using too much food, alcohol, or drugs, or watching too much television. Our aim is to stay tuned to our process, not to escape it.

Staying attuned will make you a deeper, more compassionate person. You will be much more sensitive to others because you feel more loving. I have invariably seen that when love is blocked in one direction, other people can benefit from the love we can give them. To get out of yourself and channel the love energy in another direction is very useful.

When an outer relationship is impossible or unrequited, it is all too common to feel humiliated or rejected. Blaming oneself or the other is destructive and useless. When the need to have the other gets too bad, it is helpful to visualize one's longing as a precious liquid that is to be corked within the bottle of oneself for a while. It will be a bad and lonely time at first but then the boiling inside will simmer down. As self-control and nonindulgence become a habit, a new image or perspective will come along to help. Then one can open up again and see what new connection with the person can be made.

In the meantime it's important to let the fantasies feed you. Don't cut them off. The popular tendency is to say, I must get over this person, I must not think about him or her, but that only represses the good energy that the attraction created. It's like turning against your own self. Fantasies will certainly come up about past lovers too, even though we are no longer in any outer relationship with them. In order to nourish the Inner Lover bond, let the fantasies roll. Think, reflect, and dream, despite the fact that outer reality does not correspond to inner desires. The images free you from the obsession with feelings.

Notice what the fantasies are saying about your attraction to the person. For instance, if you are attracted to a spiritual leader or teacher of any kind, your intense desire-is certainly about developing your own abilities and strengths in certain ways. If you fall in love with a physics or literature teacher, pursue physics or literature more, not the teacher.

When we fantasize about another person, we literally incorporate them. We take their qualities into our body and mind. The qualities suffuse us invisibly, but quite effectively. That's why so many dreams, images, or fantasies are sexual in nature. There is no stronger graphic or symbolic image than that of two beings coming together physically. Every time there is an imaginative union a great deal of inner fertilization is taking place. When we spontaneously receive such images, our inner male and female figures are in harmony, a state of being which will find its expression in one's outer life as well. To deny such images because they don't correspond with outer reality is to block off the creative possibilities that the person represents. If we can embrace our projections, we will get much further on the path of individuation.

It's as if the other person represents a great feast, and bit by bit we eat up the offering. When we've finished the feast, we will move on to another. This idea of a person as a rich source of food for one to take in is paradoxical because on the outer level one probably feels extremely deprived, as though the goodies are being withheld. Many of us feel very empty inside. When we partake of an Inner Lover, we fill up the void. By tapping into this generous source we become full in a way we would never experience with the person in an outer relationship.

Dreams are the Inner Lover's playing fields. Free-flowing inner dialogues are also important. (See part five, "How to Use Inner Lover Fantasies.")

An example of an inappropriate relationship is a man who fell in love with his mate's best friend from college. He was in a quandary over what to do. For him to act on the attraction would likely sever the woman's bond with her friend, not to mention his own with her. He would bring plenty of guilt into the new liaison, which would not bode well. Three relationships could be jeopardized. So, instead, he allowed his life to be enriched by watching where his fantasies of this woman led, which ultimately turned out to be a new career. He established a business concerned with environmental protection, work that was far more meaningful to him than his previous job. The content of his life changed dramatically. He was far more secure about himself and his own goals. His partner adjusted to the changes, attracted to his newfound purposefulness.

The ultimate in impossible relationship is when a beloved dies, and one is forced to be without the physical presence of the other. Images of the person as an Inner Lover can serve one very well in the mourning process.

One widower used his loneliness and memories as fuel to write a children's book based on his wife's character. A woman, who took to thinking of her deceased partner as an Inner Lover, wrote me that doing so gave her a "great sense of peace and wholeness and a renewed sense of her presence with me. . . . I feel like we are together within one body—my body—which is all there is left on this earth plane. The thought makes me smile inside and out. I feel so filled with the love we share."

A woman whose husband died at age thirty-nine within a month of diagnosis describes her experience with him as an Inner Lover before and after he died.

When he was alive, he would motivate things I do. I'd write songs for him. I felt freer than I had ever to express myself artistically without being judged. He awaited eagerly to hear whatever I created and he'd love it. I was able to internalize his feelings for me.

After he died, I went through photographs to try to recapture myself through the way he saw me. It's been five months and I dream about him every night. Sometimes I believe the dreams are messages from him, sometimes that they are about him within myself.

I also felt his presence very strongly in his parents' house after the funeral. His former wife was there—she still loved him even though she hadn't seen him in ten years. She hugged me and whispered in my ear, as if she was coming from a different level: "He will give you the strength you need. Let him help you." He has given me strength. I look to his spirit for that.

Once I asked him just to point me in a direction. I felt guided to Peter Matthiessen's *The Snow Leopard*. In it his wife is dying of cancer and the Buddhists say prayers for the survival of her soul.

Once I felt his spirit physically embrace me. I felt warm and happy.

In making a new life, this woman internalized the best values that he represented, and she has let her love guide her. Death may end a life, but not a relationship. In the future she will very likely glean more meaning from her bond with him.

Life is meant to be deep and ecstatic. It is not necessary to cut off the possibilities for ourselves. We are meant for more joy, although getting it sometimes means a sidetrip through excruciating loss. Inner Lovers carry us toward peaceful ecstasy in our lives, if we let ourselves be embraced and carried more and more on the erotic tide.

Reverberations of a Brief Encounter

While the one-night stand usually gets a bad rap, my (one-day) encounter with Tom was a blessing in disguise. He appeared when I was in the death throes of my marriage. Because of the brevity of my actual contact with the man, the Inner Lover images that he sparked are easy to see in operation. He would never know the role he played for me. So it is with many of us, particularly in times of transition.

Tom was our veterinarian. I happened to run into him the last night my husband and I went out together. We were at a local country and western roadhouse, and Tom asked me to dance. He suddenly seemed handsome, muscular, and earthy.

I hadn't been so excited about an available man in years, so I shakily called him and asked if he would like to meet me for a drink. He said yes, he would very much. He had been shy of calling me because I was married.

We met and had a few strong drinks, which probably clouded my seeing the real person for what he was. He told me about flying his own airplanes, scuba diving, riding his motorcycle, raising cattle, and lifting weights. Outside the bar he kissed me and asked me to go home with him. I declined, but we set a date for me to go over to his house soon after.

He was an adventurer, a clear image of strength and animal vitality that was so lacking in me at that time. I learned later that he was also a drug abuser and womanizer. An outer relationship with him would have been very unhappy, I'm sure, but on an inner level he gave me force and courage to enter a new phase of my life.

I went to his house in early spring for our rendezvous. Over a glass of wine, he bluntly said that he had no one in his life with whom the sex was any good, nor did he want to feel tied to anyone. On his dresser in front of a picture of his children was a gold medallion inscribed "always" (I surmised it was from one of the women he wouldn't want to be bound to but who obviously hoped otherwise). He asked me what was exciting about my life. Basically, because of the breakup of my family, I felt like an empty sack. I was not brave enough to tell him that.

We spent the afternoon in bed. At dusk we rose and dressed. He kissed me and said he would call.

I went home, lay down on the couch, and let the episode start to wash over me. The next day I wrote:

So there he was. She saw him standing in the field, the shorn earth laid out as far as the eye could see in any direction, a bunch of cattle gathered together nearby, his stalwart barn, his eye out for fox, woodchuck, hawk. And then they are in his house, which he designed with a huge wood-burning stove and the rooms so that there is an open flow from the kitchen to the dining area to the living room, bedroom, and dressing room. And he is standing there, looking at her with bright eyes, his brawny chest and shoulders bulging beneath his dark blue flannel shirt, his stomach, buttocks, and legs firm and muscled. He is talking about his planes and the thrill of stunt flying and then about a song he loves in which an Indian finds peace in life only after he is shot down, and she is affected that his eyes are warm and appreciative. His face is tanned. A short beard rims his cheeks. When he kisses her, she feels the bristle and his hands pressing her tightly and her mouth eager for his.

As they make love, she sees around them the trees, the animals, the sky, sun, moon, and stars. As they act on the life instinct

between them, she feels connected to the universe, to that creative force underlying them all, which is after all life itself. She sees
herself spread-eagled on the rolling turf, nearby wild brambles
and a brook making its winding way over rocks and roots. When
he comes to enter her body, he is half-man, half-horse, a cen-
taur, Poseidon with a dolphin on his shoulder, primitive shaggy
potency. Oh yes he has a high regard for her. There is no question
of respect here. And she, as her skin blends with the earth, she
cries aloud for him, never wanting anything more in her life than
to be taken over by him, ravished, impregnated not with a child
but his energy.

It is a copulation that brings her back from the valley of death,
that awakens in her the desire to live, that fills her with the pain
of longing and total vulnerability to the demands of destiny.

She has become transparent and yielding as a cloud. She is
floating away, having given herself over, let go. She has reached
into the genitals of the underground, flung and beat herself upon
the wet throbbing tissues, trembled violently, and shuddered in
the fecundity of it all. Because of him, the fire blazes. She will live.

In this rhapsody the man and the situation were already transformed into a primal, even mythological or archetypal encounter.
Through him I united with a vital force in the Self that was to be
the most life-engendering event to sustain me at the end of my
marriage. Despite all my machinations to try to see him again, it
was not to be. The point of the encounter most emphatically was
not to be found in an outer bond. He was a bridge to transpersonal
layers of my unconscious, although I didn't know it yet.

Thus, during the time I was despairing over the divorce, I was
also feeding on healing sexual fantasies. In an early one I collapsed in his presence as if the power and strength in his mascu-
linity enabled me to utterly let go, after being so responsible and
stiff-shouldered in my marriage. I pictured us lolling nude in the
sun or my dancing for him, exciting him enormously. I envisioned
talking to him about my fantasies and his being in awe of how
much meaning I saw in life.

I projected onto him my desire to be seen as strong and important. I still believed I had to get this recognition from the man

and felt deprived because he was not with me. Since he hadn't called me, hadn't zoomed toward me like a bee to a flower, I was certain there was something wrong with me.

As the days passed, I dwelled on his brawny, dark, bearded, close-to-animal aspects. Obviously these were what I lacked and needed to take in. Also, I began to notice that every time I imagined us making love, a bar such as at a railroad crossing, would cross my vision (this seemed to be a warning that this relationship would go nowhere).

I began to think about the limitations of the real man. He had told me that his sister, business partner, and dog had died recently. He'd also had a second divorce and a major operation. I could see how this man could want to stay unattached but I wanted to pound his chest for not pursuing me. I was so afraid that if I didn't have him, I would lose access to his animal power.

Because I now was more alert to the Inner Lover dynamic, I paid more attention to it, cultivating it rather than feeling victimized by not having the lover. In my journal work on the situation I would dialogue with him, as well as with the relationship, my body, and Inner Wisdom figures. In a dialogue with the relationship, it said that he was not sensitive to me, would not see nor feel me clearly. He was into sensation, not soul-searching, and I was responding to the active side of him because that's what I needed to draw me outside of my shell. He was "the apple of life" and now that I'd taken a bite, I couldn't go back to the way things were again. I would have to be on my own—with or without him I would have to make my own way.

In a dream *I am in a waiting room, trying to hide a bloody towel* (my hurt and longings). *Tom is the dentist and he's working on my daughter's teeth.* My daughter represents for me independence of spirit, sexual and otherwise, and so I figured that my fantasies about Tom had to do with the work I was doing in getting the strength I needed to live on my own and bite through the necessary situations.

Since Aphrodite is the goddess who initiates sexual attractions, I turned to her for insight. In a journal dialogue she pointed out how he had been turned on by me but was deterred by my still being married, a possibility I'd probably not thought of because I was so worried about being rejected. She told me that he thinks before he leaps, and I leap and then think. She instructed me about making allowances for the different ways people perceive events. (This is a good example of how inner dialogues correct and balance one's attitudes.)

I told her that if the relationship was not to be, I wished she'd bring the experiment to an end. She said that while I don't like to be hurt, hurting can open doors as much as loving can.

In my journal I gushed to my fantasy lover, whom I was so hungry for after the meager fare during the last years of my marriage:

> Last night I had this vision of you in my heart—it was glowing with light. I see us in bed, my body shuddering with desire and then as if my skin shed, I become like an attacking animal, and you are taken aback. I am afraid of hurting you if I let go like that; maybe only in fantasy is it safe.
>
> I want to kiss your penis and swallow it. Kiss between your legs, make your chest ripple. I'd like to drive you crazy. I'd like to feel I had the power to do that. I'd like to treat our union royally, a sacred happening. I'd like to really roll and beat and sweat over us. I'd like to feel you strong enough to take me and feel you craving as I do.
>
> I carry you deep inside me. You are part of my identity.

After my husband left the house, I also felt anger, which I used to help me, to plan and take charge of the furnace, the electricity, and plumbing system for the first time. I had to pay the bills and balance the budget, and at the same time cope with the tangled legal and financial negotiations of a divorce.

As Tom did, I rented out stalls in my barn to two horse owners for extra income. I always liked being around horses and now valued even more the physicality of digging straw and manure, the nickering of horses over the fence, stroking their dusty necks, seeing their bright eyes, and serene grazing. I also had several gardens to care for and drew sustenance from planting, weeding, and philosophizing about them.

I still had a hard time letting go of the real man and thus needed to do more journal work to see what more I needed to learn.

In a dream *Tom lives next door to me across an expanse of lawn. I sneak up to his room and find him sleeping there. He is wearing pyjamas of a wonderfully vivid forest green. I take his captain's hat.* Taking his hat, I assumed the symbol of his power for myself The man in green is an archetypal image for nature powers. This image would grow in importance for me over the years.

I have a series of Self images: *a stream running underground—a snake slithers in from the left—it is yellow and green, tongue flashing— I like it and lay with it and kiss it—it goes into my vagina and leaves three eggs as though my vagina is its nest—the eggs hatch and fledglings cheep madly for food—then I see the diamond-hard eye of an eagle— then the bright warm innocent eyes of the dead owl I'd found—they were burning bright with love and awe of the world (wind, earth, plumage) even though they meet cold and death.*

About a year after the first encounter with him, I began to see a darker facet of the obsession. Aside from being attracted to his managerial and adventurous sides, I thought about his addiction to alcohol and drugs as an escape from his own hells and wondered whether or not I too had wanted to escape from the grief I was experiencing. Within a short time I decided to stop drinking altogether, one of the best steps I've ever taken.

In a journal dialogue when I once again beseeched an Inner Wisdom figure for help, I was told:

"I want you to be tougher, not soft and squishy, submissive and docile. Don't be in those insecurities."

"But what do I do when they come?"

"Be vulnerable. You are scared to be really vulnerable. Just do it more. It will benefit everything you do. Your pain and anger with your mother and stepfather caused you to withdraw and surround yourself with a shell. You are free from that environment now." (While I could take some first steps in being more vulnerable, each time felt like being sliced with a razor blade.)

"Do my prayers make a difference?"

"Yes, they do but the way is not clear. I know your desires. I want you to feel that intensity and find the channels for it. There are rivers and tributaries. Eventually you will find a channel for your energy, and that is what I want you to find. Right now you are to build your self. See yourself as a horse. Strong, fiery, passionate, docile sometimes, shy, self-protective, hungry, playful, mean, biting, kicking, rhythmical."

"But what do I do about my suffering?"

"Disregard it. I am moving you."

I also tried dialoguing with the half-man, half-horse god that I'd first fantasized copulating with after being with Tom. I called him Tishnar after a character in a story by Anaïs Nin, wherein she says Tishnar meant dream lover. (This is an example of an Inner Wisdom dialogue as described in part five).

"I'm excited to address you for the first time. I smile and laugh when I think of you. I also get quite overwhelmed by your erotic power. You must know how much I love and cherish you?"

"But you starve me!"

"How can I feed you?"

"Open the door and let me run around. I am strong and protective. I can take you places."

(I see him as a wild white horse.) "Where do you want me to go first?"

"Talk to me. Spend time with me so we get to know each other. Keep your longings with me. Let the other people go free. Take them as they come. Express your desires freely. But come to me when your heart hurts."

"Am I going to get pregnant with this fucking?"

"You are already pregnant with desires and inklings, like little green shoots."

"You mean my desires are not the source of all misery as the Buddhists say?"

"No, they are the flowers that lead you on. Pluck them and make bouquets."

"Will I suffer a lot?"

"No, you will have great understanding." I muse about the dark center of the earth and animal instincts. He says, "That is just the beginning. We eat, sleep, fight, and fuck. Honor those in your life. Give them pre-eminence now."

105

"I could express myself more. There is more flow, more energy building, more power building, like a stream down a mountain." (I see myself laughing excitedly, listening, vibrating, being *myself*.) "I really like this feeling but with other people I seem to lose it."

"No, you activate them. That's why they desire you. They want your energy. Give and also stay in tune with me."

"It's wonderful when two people can get together who have their own sources. Then they can give and not demand. They know how to take care of themselves. I wish I could live that."

"You can. Just trust me. Stay with me. I am faithful."

I kept returning to the dreadful ache of my body and feeling embarrassed by its neediness.

Tishnar said, "Unfulfilled sex becomes smoke or spirit. The flame burns. It becomes smoke—transparent in the process of consuming you. You need to burn."

"For what?"

"Color and richness."

And so my inner burning eventually manifested in changes in my outer life. For instance, to my surprise a friend of mine, who had a house on Tortola, in the Virgin Islands, offered it to me for a week free. I thought the opportunity was too good to pass up, so I went down there and learned to scuba dive. That trip led to other diving expeditions, introducing me to the magnificent underwater world around coral reefs. Like Tom, I became a certified scuba diver. Although I didn't do it with him, diving became a treasured adventure for me.

Later the Inner Lover figure of Tom appeared in a dream as a dive master who led me through congested waters (a common motif). First he took me to a cave to copulate and then to examine some dead bodies from my past. Through dialogues I drew on his superhuman strength for the protection I needed as I descended into personal material buried in my unconscious. The water would clear as I relived past moments. Thus, while Tom the person was barely in my life, as an Inner Lover he became a soul guide.

A woman tells me about an encounter with a man to whom she was very attracted, although she ended up marrying his best friend. The man, John, nevertheless has appeared in her dreams over the years whenever she gets into some difficulty. I asked her what she liked about him.

"He was a feminist. He was the first man who appreciated my intellect and made me feel I was interesting. He had a lot of depth and understanding of life, was very grounded in his body. He was the first man I told my feelings to."

She has a recurring dream of him that varies slightly. "He is coming for a short visit, and there is always the question whether I have enough food for him and how long will he stay. I always want him to stay and feel horrified when he goes. When he's there, I feel a wholeness in my life, and I feel a sense of resting in myself. One thing I always admired and would like to incorporate is his belief in himself separate from what our culture asks. He's a curator of folklore in a museum and yet never completed his B.A.; he's not intimidated around Ph.D.'s either. I like his sense of personal authority that doesn't need to be validated externally. I talk to him about how he would deal with the situation I'm in.

People frequently say about love objects with whom they've had the briefest of contact that the relationship happens on another level. One woman describes how in regard to a certain man, she dreamed of kissing him and getting a hook in her mouth. That hook stayed with her for several years, although the actual man was quite distant. Although it felt sometimes like the hook would drag her through hell forever, in the process she gained color, originality, and independence. She would not trade that experience for anything.

In part four of this book, "The Wedding," I will discuss more precisely the rewards for tending the hearth of the Inner Lover. So far I've wanted to show the many ways Inner Lover images appear to take us on journeys.

In the next chapter I describe another Inner Lover process that illustrates the importance of every unique step along the way, despite the seeming complications. At the very least one can see how valuable passion is, regardless of what is happening in the actual relationship. People often miss all they can get out of life and each other by demanding that all fulfillment and satisfaction come from the outer connection immediately. Passion becomes far more than sexual intensity. It means openness of one's soul to receive energies that are beyond possible comforts with another. We need to be strong enough to daily align with them, contain, and eventually embody them. Make a nest for nurturing your passion.

Eros and Timing

The narratives about my experiences with Alan the therapist and Tom the adventurer illustrate how most of the activity took place in my imagination and how it was linked to soul development. The stories are two examples in which the outer events played less of a part than they would with couples who are together daily. Obviously it is easier to illustrate Inner Lover dynamics with such examples, but it's important to realize that the same principles apply to couples who are with each other regularly. For such couples, a problem may be not having enough distance to allow the imagination to play its role.

To some readers immersed in co-dependency literature, like Robin Norwood's *Women Who Love Too Much*, the foregoing accounts of relationships might seem to be the kind they want to avoid because of the intense emotions engendered, such as anger, fear, hurt. Norwood acknowledges that people try very hard to recreate situations they had as a child, but her remedy is to advise the reader to unequivocally stop. She ignores the psychological fact that we are driven to recreate the past in order to heal ourselves. As adults we can accomplish in our love bonds what we could not accomplish as a small powerless child. To reject such opportunities is to dam the river of life, which results in turning against oneself.

When you are conscious of your obsessive longings, for instance, and feel them to the nth degree (drinking the cup to the dregs, as Jung once said), they will live a natural life and evolve positively. Even, to take the worst case, if you are attracted to a betrayer and a thief and get really burned by the experience, you will be careful to avoid such people again. You will want to treat yourself better.

In the "Parent" chapters in part two I discussed negative imprinting in early childhood experience. If you have low self-esteem, you will have both inner and outer figures in your life who reflect that attitude. Having been abused, in particular, will eventually make one miserable enough and result in enough anger to instigate change. Those who have been sexually abused by parents, for instance, say that when they can get to the rage, they begin to recover. In the souls of such people are helpful Inner Lovers, for one of the characteristics of the unconscious is to send up compensating images that you need to correct the imbalances in your life. Thus, paying attention to Inner Lover figures can rescue you from the worst of situations.

It does not make any difference whether you are with or without a partner for soul work to be accomplished. The important point is becoming aware of what kinds of figures are inside and what they have to say about where your life is going. In my case I had long and short relationships, some that were physically fulfilled and some that were not. A paradox is that despite my longing for physical fulfillment, great intensities along other lines built up in me when I did not receive it. Being alone is a time for really drawing close to the nourishing figures inside. Thus the absence of an outer lover can be as fulfilling as the presence of one.

One reason then I offer the stories of Alan, Tom, and now Paul is to show how valuable and yet paradoxical the anguish of suffering is. I was never beaten or raped and yet I—and many others like me—felt tortured (again, possible whether you are with someone or not). During the torment of obsession or conflict with another, one's Inner Lovers appear in various forms that instruct us about our lives, as I try to show. More than that, however, they are forming a center within us that enables us to endure the storms of life more solidly. When chaos or a desert surrounds you, like a tree you send roots deep into the Self for nourishment. These roots hold you firmly in place. Thus, being buffeted strengthens your will, just as when the body is invaded by a virus, it grows stronger in self-defense.

So, while some of my stories may seem to involve disappointment and loss, they illustrate how I was being transformed into a much more powerful person in the process. The experiences contained a great deal of meaning. We talk about commitment as if it means only staying with another person. However, commitment to a process that is alive with feeling, thought, and fantasy is just as important. So is commitment to oneself and paying attention to Inner Lovers as well as outer ones.

Surely, the reader has been disappointed in love. Do you see those experiences as failures? If so, you are doing yourself a great injustice. Better to be honest with yourself and accept your thoughts, feelings, and fantasies about others as they are and as they come, however inconvenient and seemingly unwanted. To do so is to have real courage. And to reap the real rewards.

Certainly one of the most frustrating aspects of love relationships concerns timing and reciprocity. It never seems as if two people are equally loving at the same moment, for we are important to each other in different ways. C. S. Lewis, for instance, lived with a woman for years but did not feel passion toward her until she was sick and dying of cancer. As a child, he had watched his mother die; it apparently took a similar situation with a loved one to open up his soul to deeper feeling. We can't predict when or how a fissure for passion will break through. Depending on our states of being, our responses to love differ. Unfortunately as couples we fight about reciprocity, despite knowing we can't be on the same wavelength at all times, perhaps at any time.

An appreciation of timing and its subtleties is crucial to love. Not only are our responses sometimes out of synch, but also a relationship itself lightens and darkens in intensity. It has its own rhythm and pace to be attuned to. In a long relationship the outer aspects change and die off more than once, in order to allow it to grow fresh leaves. Each partner is on a journey of individuation and needs to test out roads privately. Being with our Inner Lovers at such times may make others' paths easier to accept.

Attractions that begin at one point in time, are interrupted for various reasons, and then resume years later represent remarkable examples of the power in timing. Such attractions contain seeds that are not ripened and harvested until many other experiences have occurred in between.

As will be seen below, timing in my relationship with Paul was important, because long dormant seeds were given a chance to sprout and grow. The romance with Paul was also significant because when we remet, he was involved with another woman, which provoked the (frequently seen) issue of an Inner Lover choosing another instead of oneself.

I first met Paul in college the spring I was a sophomore and he a junior. He was slight, quick, and brainy with pale gentle eyes and an angelic face. He did not tell me then but his mother had somehow been mentally disturbed during her pregnancy with him and had been put into an institution by the time he was three. He'd been "boarded out" with a few families until he was old enough to go to school and live with his father. In his teens he'd been sent to a prestigious boarding school, and then he won a scholarship to an ivy league college.

I have a memory of one Sunday afternoon in May when the magnolia trees were in full radiant pungent bloom. Intoxicated, I climbed the low branches of the tree to reach for a blossom. I extended myself too far and in reaching out for this beauty, suddenly fell to the ground. I lay dazed and injured and empty-handed. This memory is a good metaphor for what happened between us.

We dated a few times. I have another memory of one night lying on him in a private room at the fraternity house, kissing feverishly.

He said, "Kiss me with abandon."

"I am," I said huskily, searching his eyes for how he could not know.

He laughed and squirmed away. "You're crushing me."

"Sorry." I rolled off to the side. I realized how much I wanted him, how willing I was to end my virginity.

But he did not take me. Then I had to go home for summer vacation. I left with the foreboding that he would find someone else because it would be too hard to sustain our connection over the long summer.

In June and July he wrote me six letters—long ones full of stories and mental flights, very little about himself. In August the letters tapered off.

When college resumed, we got together and had an intense reunion. And then he did not call again. On the brink of consummation he dropped out of contact. I could not understand how or why anyone would back away from that flame. Time eventually buried him in a remote pocket of my psyche. Later that year I met Brian.

Some twenty years later Paul and I reconnected. In the meantime I had married, raised two children, and divorced. Paul had gone on to get a Ph.D., spent some years teaching, and now made political documentaries for television. In his senior year at college he'd met someone whom he later married; they had two daughters. Paul said they did not communicate intimately and after thirteen years she left him for another man. The shock of her leaving devastated him; it must have been all too reminiscent of losing his mother. Furthermore, she tried to move with their daughters to another state across the country. But he fought back—and won.

After the divorce, he saw many women, even coming close to marrying one. Then he met Maud, a dancer. They had been together five years—all the while maintaining separate apartments—when I appeared. Maud was extraverted and did not infringe on his time. He said (alarming to me) that he had complete power over her.

After my divorce I'd been on a long job search. I'd seen Paul's name in a journal I subscribed to and wrote him a networking letter, asking if he could give me advice. He responded warmly, inviting me to meet him at the office and to go out for dinner.

When I saw him, I was astonished at how much he still resembled my memory of him. He was still slim and forceful, though his hair was thinner. Walking together to a Japanese restaurant, I was amazed to be with him again after two decades of separation.

Over dinner we filled each other in on the details of the past. He said, "You know back then I didn't want to get serious. Or involved. I was afraid of being hurt. I didn't have the nerve to explain it to you."

"I was hurt," I murmured.

"I'm very glad to see you now."

"That was a long time ago."

"I've changed a lot since then."

"Have you?" I wondered.

"I was afraid of my emotions. I try not to be now. With Maud I have established more closeness than I had with my wife."

I was growing increasingly aware of desire for him building in my gut and loins. I was so astonished and alarmed I didn't know what to do or say to him. When we parted, I felt my whole body ring and vibrate as though a gong deep within me had been struck. Oh God, I thought, what am I in for? The pocket in which Paul had been secreted away was now turned inside out and exposed.

By the way, a sure sign of the Inner Lover aspect of any relationship is the deep resonance in one's body. Being physically excited to the very nerve endings of one's fingers and feeling that this is more than one can handle show how one's psyche is being altered. Some people interpret this unusual level of arousal as too overwhelming. They mistakenly feel out of control, as if the other is taking them over. Many of us fear these sensations, but they represent the intensity of life in its promise of abundance. One fears one's heart will be broken. The paradox is that one's heart is sure to be "broken open," even if the outer relationship develops and lasts over time. One's metaphorical heart or capacity for love must be expanded in order to appreciate the mystery of life. When one's body vibrates, one can receive an intuitive flash that this relationship will be meaningful in one's future, as I did.

After that dinner with Paul, I dreamed *Paul and I are eating a bowl of insects coated with purple syrup until they get too big and awful.* I connected the purple syrup with purple passion and the insects with a primal level of communication. When the insects were small, they were easier to eat than when they got big. Eventually I would face having to bite through the big ones.

A week later he called and asked if I would help him in the research and production of a nature film. Yes, of course, I would.

And so began several years of work and shared lunches, which framed the saga of our creative relationship. The controlled circumstances were fertile ground, ideal for Inner Lover development.

I was infused with erotic warmth and joy, at times afraid it would take me over. In my journal I wrote what would turn out to be a leitmotif: "I wonder if I am capable of using my love for him and not trying to possess him or feel hurt. In other words, can I carry the Inner Lover part for me, whether he feels the same or not?"

Paul arranged for me to meet Maud, "to ground that relationship in reality." I went feeling petrified but attempted to be warm and friendly.

Maud lived in a studio apartment. When we entered, she was facing the mirror, combing out long black wet hair. She wore a pink leotard with a burlap vest. He went to her, and she looked at him for approval. When Maud nodded at me, I felt appraised and excluded.

At a counter facing the stove and refrigerator were some high stools. Paul sat on one. I did likewise. Paul nibbled on some nuts without offering me any. They talked about marketing Maud's work while she cooked shrimp and noodles.

We sat around a small table to eat. Maud served Paul, stroking his arm when she handed him his plate. She was warm and demonstrative, where he was cool and commanding. I left as soon as I could. My parting glimpse was of Paul, standing with his hands in his pockets, grinning guiltily at me before turning to Maud.

In a dream *Paul comes up behind me and presses himself against me. I feel great arousal and lift my dress and spread my legs to receive him.* While on the outer level I was experiencing an opening up to my connection with him, I also had to see this lover Paul as a warming, unifying factor in my psyche. The loving I was getting inside made me be more receptive to his qualities. It also kept me riveted to him.

One spring day I said to Paul, "I don't think I can be just friends with you. I am all the time wanting you in the old way. It's very hard for me."

"If I started anything with you, Maud would leave me." He explained how he was against having any affair in secret because he thought that was destructive. He also thought that if he saw me just for a short fling, I'd be too upset.

Even while proposing an affair to Paul, I was wrestling with doubts about my infringing on his relationship with Maud. At first as a feminist I had been opposed to invading another woman's territory. But then as my desire persisted, he became more important to me than my principle about her. This coming to accept and even fight for my wishes became an important psychological milestone. It meant I didn't back off from my passion.

Meanwhile we were working more and more closely together, and Paul was very pleased with the results. We were both committed to the same causes and much of our conversation flowed along those lines. I had a satisfying dream in which *I appear plain and stocky and awkward. Paul comes in jauntily, wearing white underwear. He kisses and holds me, saying he loves me. I feel good. I say I know my kids like him too. We all feel loose together. He says he loves this plain woman too. I am happy.* I was coming to accept my homeliest aspects and be more playful.

I concentrated on adding his wildness, imagination, and force to my repertoire. But I longed for his real body. We'd be sitting side by side and I'd want to touch his small hand or crush my chest against his. It didn't seem fair that life was presenting me with him in order to be rejected all over again.

I had a dream in which *I am calling him to bed. He is irritable and afraid because his defenses are down and that gives me a lot of power. He has said he will love me. He will love me instead of Maud. He could be hurt but he has opted to trust, and I am not sure I am a good caretaker of him.*

Dreams like this are tricky. They need to be seen in two dimensions. On the outer level, it was possible that someday he could love me instead of Maud, although it was not manifested at the present time. On an inner level, it is about my male lover coming to prefer me and trusting that, although there is some question as to whether I will be sensitive and loyal enough. Again and again I was cautioned inwardly to develop more trust and caring for my Inner Lover, which could be translated to mean my own creativity and power.

Nevertheless I was plunged into pain repeatedly. On my birthday he offered to buy my lunch. I said no and asked for a hug, but he refused, saying he was against public displays of affection or the suggestion that it would mean something he didn't intend.

My dreams insisted that I speak my feelings no matter what. I repeatedly had to summon all my courage and overcome fear of humiliation. In one dream *we are lying in separate beds in the semi-dark. I feel proud to be there but also sadly accepting the separation. Somehow he bridges the inhibition and pulls me over to make love. I lie on him with him inside me. Although I don't feel his penis tactilely, it is like I'm having orgasm at the slow deep connection. Feels very pelvic-centered and like riding a thundercloud.* I took this to mean that when I did reveal my true feelings, I would unite with my Inner Lover Paul, regardless of what was happening on the outer level.

While these dreams pressed toward an inner union, I also believe that they reflected some of Paul's unconscious erotic feeling for me. He was resistant to expressing, even feeling, love for a woman because that gave her power over him. He was even more afraid to do so with me because he wanted to stay committed to Maud.

Meanwhile I dreamed that *he wants to marry me and wants me to be patient.* The lack of correspondence between the inner and outer made me crazy. In the past he'd been unable to love me and now it seemed he was doing the same thing again. I didn't want a man like that. Yet, the lovemaking I fantasized was so intense it left me trembling.

He began to discuss fantasies of having me join them and tried to get me to get better acquainted with Maud. I cooperated to some extent but invariably I would feel overwhelmed by feelings of being excluded and jealous of his attention going to her. Then I'd be sure he didn't love me.

Week after week we'd talk about ourselves and our relationship. It was totally new to both of us to do so much erotic talking and certainly contributed to our growing security and intimacy. Normally with couples subtle feelings get silenced in sex. By having an obstacle to sex we had to express ourselves verbally much more. Our delicately nuanced talking was a real benefit for both of us. Furthermore, I was not used to actively pursuing the subject of my desires so much as being the passive recipient of someone else's. I felt more empowered to initiate and declare my love. During the process, we were becoming very good friends, helping each other in many ways. Also, even though we were not physical lovers, our bodies were suffused with the glow and well-being that love initially brings.

About this time Paul offered to call me on a regular basis to relieve my distress (he often said he was doing things for me, never himself). The first time he called me, he started off with jokes and got off the line after ten minutes. In the beginning, when he was calling once a week, he was afraid his line would be tapped, and he would not call on the weekends because he didn't want to disturb Maud. Later on he would want to call in front of Maud so as not to have any secrets, but I did not like that because I then did not feel he was talking to me so much as showing off in front of both of us. Eventually he called daily. We kept on talking until I could not stand it anymore, but that came later.

I wrote in my journal: "I want to use these calls to share myself with a man as I have not done. It is an opportunity to meet a challenge in myself and possibly create more of an intimate bond. I'd like to practice the gentle art of relationship." I also thought that maybe he was building a relationship with me indirectly, which was safer to him, the way he could more easily relate to Maud in the beginning because she was in love with someone else. Often I thought of him as a skittish deer. I kept holding out my hand, hoping someday he would trust me.

I dream *Paul is very hungry. We eat, laugh, and talk together.* During our meetings we were very absorbed in one another; yet I suffered from not knowing what would happen next. I'd remind myself that "life is a mystery to be lived, not a problem to be solved." With Paul I had to learn to be in the present moment without possessing him. I also thought that if we did not enjoy each other in a daily way, there would be no basis for anything long-lasting.

Yet the Eros in me also got frustrated and angry, particularly at the absence of touching and holding each other. One day I said, "I fantasize burning you with lighted cigarettes."

He said weakly, "I've been waiting for your anger and here it is. It does not feel pleasant."

I grew tearful, sure that this would produce an ending. But it did not, and the fact that our connection could continue erotically despite my anger was another lesson for me to learn. He did not run away but said, "I feel more for you than before."

"For a year I've been near tears every time I leave you."

"I'm sorry. Do you think you should quit?"

We would discuss my leaving but then both of us liked the way we were working together. Nor did the bond between us seem finished.

The outcome seemed less important than the need to overcome our fear of discussing painful subjects. All we had was the journey that we were on, in which every moment was an "outcome."

My sense of futility over ever having my hopes and desires fulfilled was a major theme in this story. Paul said he would not leave Maud (doth he protest too much? I would wonder). The odds seemed very much against the likelihood of my getting what I wanted. I was embarrassed about the situation with him in front of my friends because I was trusting my inner process, which few could understand. Since my dreams were never discouraging, I could not quite give him up. It seemed their message was that I should act like I had a hard impassioned penis.

Paul often spoke to me about surrendering to him, saying that he could not love until he was surrendered to. Perhaps because of his being abandoned by the original female—his mother— in infancy, he needed to be absolutely sure of a woman before he could feel safe enough to love her. Perhaps his desire for two women had to do with having both safety and the healing power of being surrounded by female energy. Or maybe it had to do simply with the love of power.

In my anger I wrote lines that ended up energizing me:

I hate you
I hate this
The truth is
You want her
You want me too
I have a drive, a hunger, a desire that won't stop
It is like a she-wolf
Fierce
Gentle
She can bite and tear and protect
How can I be fierce with Paul?
Tear into his soft body
Or protect him?
He is still sizing me up
He hasn't merged with me
He has loved but he knows when love stops
He says he loves Maud
He acts like he does
But I don't believe he does
I don't believe he loves like I do
What does a she-wolf do?
She thinks about the hunger in her gut
And she tries to fill herself
What would she do about Maud?
She would fight her
She would tear her from limb to limb
And take away her mate
My blunted teeth—my voice—are afraid
Afraid of his displeasure
So what? Maybe it's
Come to the end of the line anyway

A warrior sticks to the path
Is firm as a rock
Is there
Big and powerful and silent
A big statement
Of being
Impenetrable
Immovable
Firm and sensitive
Not thrown off course
Which is to have him
Knowing water flows
Gently but wears down
Knowing nature does its work
That he may be dumb
That we all may be dumb
But I am firm in my love
And want of him and am entitled to have it
I am confident of my right to have it

Then came my birthday in July. I threw a party just to entice him out to my house. Prior to this, he hadn't invited me to his apartment or come to my place because he was afraid to be alone with me. But he agreed to come to the party without Maud. I was extremely excited. After it was over, he stayed on for supper with my children. Sitting around talking made him think, he said, that he could have married me and we would be sitting there with our own children. But all he wanted was for me to come join him and Maud. Leaving, he gave me a kiss goodbye. I was enormously frustrated.

Shortly after, I dreamed that *he and I are standing naked and kissing in front of a very tall, green mound of earth.* Such a mound is an ancient fertility symbol. The dream indicated an abundant amount of creative energy present. And, in the years to come we would collaborate very closely in our work, sharing a mission to improve conditions in the world. Doing so opened up areas that had been closed to me before: travel, computerized video editing, science, and the politics of international conflict resolution.

I dreamed: *I am with Paul. He is leaving Maud for me. He is making love with me. It is night. I am surprised. It is most emphatic that he is there for me.* While such a dream would puzzle me, it at least would confirm my bond with the inner Paul and encourage me to continue our relationship and learn from it.

Once, when I was fearful, I dreamed that *he seizes me by the back of the neck to keep me with him.* He agreed that in a sense he did that and wanted me to stay with him.

Once in meditating over how I could persist in this agonizing situation, I received the image of his putting his hand over my heart. I took that to mean to trust my love no matter what form our partnership took.

For a while I developed an intense headache that wouldn't go away. In a session with a body therapist it came out how I couldn't stand not being physically acknowledged by Paul. I then mustered up the courage to tell Paul how overwhelmed I was by wanting him so much and how awful it was not to be affectionate with each other. Out of a strong intuition, I said, "We have something very important to give each other over the field of our bodies. Our relationship could be even more fruitful."

He spent the night (he said) tossing and turning, stirred up over my words, but too paralyzed to move away from Maud toward me even if he wanted to. His resistance was excruciating.

A dream instructed me. In it *an Indian woman adds a fish to her pelt. I ask her what the fish are and learn that they are like little currents of love or Eros. Above all, they are not to be held but allowed to glide and flow between him and me. They are seen in night thoughts, not daylight.* I felt encouraged not to worry but to watch the fish swim and appreciate them.

Two years into our relationship he said that he had had a dream in which *there is a door. On the panel above it are the three of our initials, his in the middle of mine and Maud's.* He said that if I agreed to his wishes to join him and Maud, he could see me becoming of equal importance to her. I said no, encouraging him to treat us like Inner Lovers but not to try to make us outer ones because doing so would cause too much trouble.

I dreamed *of being with him in my office. I turn into an eagle and attack him, stripping his skin to the bone. Another time the eagle picks Paul up and drops him over a cliff for having offended the father spirit.* My anger had become so great that I felt pushed into doing something major for myself. I had wanted to go to Crete for a long time; now, moreover, I would do it for a month on my own.

While I was gone, I felt I could safely experience my rage for as long as it took. I decided not to write Paul. One day I made a ritual of throwing stones at a figure of him I'd drawn on the ground in order to "kill" him off.

The volcano inside me calmed. I continued to feel love and at the very end of this trip wrote him about my longing to be passionate with him and to share a home with him, begging him to let us be lovers. That night I dreamed of saying to him, *"Do with me what you will" and he intensely fucks me.* This was the greatest surrender to my feelings I'd ever made. I felt very humbled, and my unconscious favorably responded with the as yet most complete union of the male and female within me. I had surrendered within. Soon afterward *coniunctio* or wedding images started coming to me.

When I returned, all Paul said was that he had been sad while I was away—and that was a big emotion for him. How hard it was to accept him the way he was in the moment compared to what was happening inside me!

Yet, it was not long afterward that he arranged to see me privately in his apartment, and our relationship was finally consummated. I was profoundly moved by actually being penetrated by him and having orgasms together. I felt a surge of creative fire and greater ease with the human animal I'd so longed for. Not only were ideas and energy released for both of us, but also a sense that I could have something of what I wanted, that my passion could be activating in and of itself.

As an Inner Lover for me Paul brought forth many changes. I incorporated much of his lively, focused, shrewd yet kindly ways of working with people, as well as professional and political skills. Above all, like Psyche in the myth, I'd fought to keep

Eros, despite despairing again and again. Inwardly, I'd achieved the union and the flowering of joy or *voluptas* more than once. I came to recognize that if I drifted away from the self I valued the most, dreams would show him choosing the other woman instead of me. Thus, I would be alarmed into better alignment. Paul too received benefits through sticking with our process, although less consciously than I did. His was a story of being engaged inwardly and outwardly by two different women. He suffered the conflicts of trying to bring them together in outer life rather than working with his dreams and fantasies on an interior level.

Despite the (inevitable) complications of this relationship, along the way it became "long-term," with all the usual concerns of maintaining Eros in an ongoing intimacy. As in all continuous bonds, I had to remember to separate the Inner Lover aspect from the actual personality of Paul. It's so important not to assume that the outer person is the same as one's imaginings. It's also crucial not to dismiss the imagined lover as irrelevant or false. For one's soul can be tended and nourished by the Inner Lover as well as the outer one.

Timing then is a vital factor, not only in coping with relationships reactivated after long periods of dormancy, but also in forcing one to sort inner and outer potentials and developing a sense of patience and wonder as the drama unfolds. Respect for timing can be so difficult. We want to know and decide *now*, not later.

The writer Nikos Kazantzakis understood this difficulty about timing and described an experience that profoundly struck him. He had once found a butterfly in a chrysalis and was impatient to see what it looked like. He "helped" the butterfly out but it was not really ready to emerge. Its wings had not yet formed. Because it could not fly, it hopped a short distance and was soon trampled.[1] So we too can be aware of the deadly necessity for relationships to mature in their own timing. Usually things are much more complex than they seem.

Friends and Same-Sex Liaisons

Friends and mentors can also evoke Inner Lovers. We tend generally to be friends with people of the same sex, but friends come in many forms. Friends who excite the imagination and profoundly affect our lives are those with Inner Lover significance.

We have many friends, but not all are life-changing. They may be good company, helpful in practical ways, good to talk to about problems or projects. But the ones I'm concerned with here are those with whom the collaboration produces new works and lifestyles. Usually we don't have sex with these persons; we think of them as mentors.

Helen was a friend with whom, for a time, I combusted creativity. We met in a consciousness-raising group for women artists. Tall, lithe, and elegant, she wore gold snakes around her arm and makeup (then a controversial issue). She was very articulate about her distress in moving toward a divorce and also her problems as an artist. In comparison I felt mute about such matters. She laughed crazily and had great zest. I asked her if she'd like to have lunch sometime. And we did. I was greatly excited at the prospect of being friends with her. She, I believe, appreciated my interest and eagerness to listen to her.

Right from the start our friendship focused on a project. I made a film of her printmaking in her large studio. There she would serve me salad with rose petals and tea from a glass pot, we would talk and talk about art, psychology, relationships, often for an hour a day. She introduced me to subjects I knew nothing about—for instance, the *I Ching* and mandalas.

She also suggested that I read the fiction and diaries of Anaïs Nin. I was electrified by the aura of this woman who wrote about dreams and lived in Paris and had semen dripping out of her. Anaïs became a major part of the bond Helen and I had. We organized a weekend conference for and about her, which later resulted in a book. Helen and I were ecstatic over our plans. The celebration weekend was the zenith of our creative collaborations and remained a touchstone for our friendship for years afterward. The book we produced on the event was also a celebration of bookmaking—with purple ink, many typefaces, photo-collages, and many styles of writing.

After that event we formed a publishing company, a la Nin and her Gemor Press. Our aim was to publish the work of women. Armed with our feminist values, we wanted to take control of our careers by achieving financial independence with our art. Books were a medium we both loved. Helen would contribute knowledge of type and paper, and I my editorial knowledge.

For a couple of years we often felt as if a magical spirit that no one else could catch was circulating between us. People would say (sometimes enviously) that together we glowed like light bulbs or walked on air. Our friendship was based on the excitement of being on the same wavelength. We were Inner Lovers for each other because we sparked each other's imaginations.

But the pressures of a business weighed on us eventually. At one point Helen wanted to start a separate press for her own art works, which devastated me because I felt her wish as an abandonment. She in turn was upset that I would try to restrict her in any way.

We were inept at being able to talk about the difficulties that arose between us. Finally, Helen withdrew from the press and, further upset by the end of an affair, moved to Sausalito, California.

I continued to operate the press marginally and have since produced about a dozen books.

Once the bond between us was ruptured, it has not been restored even though we have continued to correspond and visit. We became ordinary friends rather than feeders of our souls. Perhaps all one can do is be grateful for being a conduit while the state of grace lasts. It is a gift bestowed, not available on demand.

The phenomenon of the Inner Lover shows up in those we call mentors. For me, one such inspiratrice was Dr. Maria Montessori, the first woman doctor of Italy and an international educator. I raised my children under the influence of her ideas and helped start a Montessori school that still flourishes today. I did not know her personally though. A mentor whom I was fortunate to know was Anaïs Nin.

Just as June Miller was the woman she wanted to be, Anaïs was the woman I wanted to be. She cultivated a romantic and sensuous presence until the day she died. She was the intellectual companion of authoritative men like Otto Rank and René Allendy. She wanted to be a great writer, and she insisted upon doing it the personal, womanly way (about which she had a great deal to say as well). "Multiple relationships" was one of her oft-used phrases, one that put fear and envy in my heart. For at the time I was confined to a marriage and two children, and her life of stepping about with a variety of men while having a husband whom she loved seemed like an alluring but unattainable ideal.

My body was deeply stirred by my idea of her even though I had not met her (one way of knowing the Inner Lover is around). In such a state I wrote Anaïs a letter of thanks for having had the courage to publish her diaries. I asked if I could interview her for an article. A purple postcard (bearing her Pisces logo) came back and suggested we meet the next time she was in New York. That occasion turned out to be a party at the Gotham Book Mart celebrating the publication of the next volume of her diary. She sent me an invitation.

I wore one of my best dresses—a light yellow poplin—that immediately seemed plain in her presence. She had on a long clinging dress with gold lamé slippers and magenta cords woven through her upswept hair. At sixty-eight years old she was the most enticing woman in the room. She greeted me sweetly, with a soft French accent, and gave me her number to call.

Because Helen had been the one to introduce me to Nin's work, I brought her along for my first visit with Anaïs. When Anaïs was in New York City (she then lived in Los Angeles with Rupert Pole), she stayed at the Washington Square Village apartment of the man she had never divorced, Ian Hugo. The central room was given over to his film work and set off by a screen laminated with his feathery copperplate engravings. Anaïs greeted us, wearing a long black dress with a V neckline that had a gold sun pinned at the base. She served us tea with thin rounds of lemon. We talked intimately about men, art, and women's struggles. She had a way of immediately establishing heart-to-heart rapport.

I wrote an essay about her and initiated a memorable conference that brought together key people in her life, such as critic Anna Balakian, Frances Steloff, poet and publisher Daisy Aldan, poet and editor William Claire. I was impressed by the way people deluged Nin with numerous letters, journal excerpts, art works. Men and women alike were grateful to her for nurturing their creative impulses.

My contact with Anaïs continued after these projects. I published a book of her then uncollected stories, called *Waste of Timelessness and Other Early Stories*. Later this book was purchased by Ohio University Press to be sold along with other titles of hers published by Swallow Press. Anaïs died in 1977, while the book was being printed.

I have continued my relationship with Anaïs as an Inner Lover figure through dialogues in my journal, especially in regard to her ability to preserve and protect relationships. One creative result of her becoming part of my soul was that I was led to do many projects about diaries, including readings and travel tours.

One woman in my life was a friend who for a while became a lover. She was a big mannish-looking woman with an easygoing, warm way. The breakup of my family, the death of my father, and the disappointment in my male therapist and the experience with Tom had left me in a wrecked state, that's for sure, and perhaps very discouraged with men. I got from her physical nurturing in a way I'd never received. I dreamed about her as a nurse tending me. She also had much to teach me in the realm of orgasmic delights. She engendered a closeness I'd not before known. She was responsive to my problems, soft and tender toward my feelings.

While our bond had difficulties, the inner gifts can be distinguished. Her solace and care restored me to being glad to be alive again. We took wonderful trips together. She taught me about being at ease and just playing. I sometimes wonder if these gifts are unique to being loved by a woman. Later I found myself returning them to men.

The bottom line in our alliances with members of either sex is the intensity of the attraction, which is what arouses the Inner Lover. The Inner Lover stays around as long as there is a lesson to be learned or a gift to be given.

Sometimes the image of an Inner Lover goes dormant for a while only to make a reappearance at a time when that quality or dynamic is needed in one's life. (We are usually drawn to particular aspects of a person, more than the whole.) Sometimes one may regret the absence of a certain Inner Lover who had once been so numinous. In those cases one can call up his or her image in meditations, though the psyche rarely goes long without sending dreams of some past or present lover. Images of power animals may appear as well; these carry Inner Lover messages, as is discussed more fully in part five, "How to Use Inner Lover Fantasies."

It's also possible, by the way, to be involved in one or more outer connections while engaged with an entirely different Inner Lover or two, as was the case when I was involved with these women. The Inner Lover aspect will pick up on what the soul needs. Such is the spice of the inner life.

PART FOUR

The Wedding

Inner Marriage

When Eros rescued Psyche after all her trials, remember, the god married the human and their child was Voluptas, or joy. Joy could be described as a state of voluptuous ecstasy, a surrendering to grace that cannot be willed into being, only received when it happens. In the introduction and the chapter on Psyche and Eros I have touched on the inner marriage; now I want to concentrate more on the meaning of this wedding and its offspring. For after all the travails, this is the bliss, the treasure, the happiness we so long for, the fulfillment of our desires. This portion of the book, then, is about the gifts we receive from attending the Inner Lover in our souls.

In the foregoing chapters about Alan the therapist, Tom the adventurer, and Paul the coworker, we saw how I was forced by circumstances to learn about the distinctions between the inner fantasies and the actual person. With all three of these men I experienced unions of sorts and creative fertilization but it was not until my relationship with Paul that I came to a more complete union and inner marriage. At this moment I surrendered most humbly to my feelings (despite abjection and possible rejection), and my psyche responded with a dream of orgasmic copulation. In this dream I experienced not just partial penetration. We were clasped in a full-length embrace. His engorged penis was solidly and comfortably ensconced in my liquid vagina, and our bodies were vibrating and throbbing their way to orgasm and beyond. This image was important because it was not just foreplay but a complete union of male and female. It could also be seen as Eros coming to join Psyche when she was nearly succumbed to death.

After this dream, images of weddings came to me. I made my bedroom a wedding bower with white lace canopy, satin sheets, white rose bouquet and ribbons in celebration of love, creation, dance, music, desire, and beauty. The point is that when images of weddings or marriages come to us in dreams or fantasies, on a soul level they represent the joining together of important conscious and unconscious parts of our personality. This union, which was called *coniunctio* by ancient alchemists (and Jung) is mediated by our Inner Lovers. In Jungian terms we have attained a balance between our egos and our anima or animus figures, who are most often evoked by our projections. When such a union takes place, the most powerful creative forces within us are unleashed. One can't force such unions. They have to happen through inner readiness. Caring for one's Inner Lovers will pave the way.

The Drive for Consummation

Dreams contain a variety of marriage or *coniunctio* motifs. Because sexual joining is such a graphic and powerful representation of physical and spiritual union (remember, the body is psyche), the unconscious often uses sexual imagery. Wedding imagery perhaps says more about devotion and commitment. Sexual and wedding images can be read as signs of one's psychological progress. Frequently dreams present a story about a wedding or sexual encounter and point to the reasons why it cannot be consummated. It's important to notice these signals from the unconscious, for they indicate what one needs to work on.

For example, a certain man frequently appeared in one woman's dreams as a lover, though in outer life they were friends and lived far apart. In one of her dreams a wedding was taking place but not for the two of them. She told him how she loved him but could never marry him. He understood and was going to help her go where she could meet many men and find the one she could marry.

In its precise way her psyche foretold her future. She would be led to a new realm of her life, wherein he would no longer play a role. She would find another Inner Lover to marry.

The woman whose husband had died (described in the chapter on impossible lovers in part three) experienced what she called an eternal wedding. "I was meditating and found myself in a chapel, where M. and I were to be married again. It was understood that this was to be on a spiritual plane, in another dimension. We exchanged rings and renewed our vows. About that time I bought a ring that had an infinity symbol on it. I felt that this vision meant our love was boundless."

This marriage gave her a great sense of peace and bonding with her departed husband. Interestingly, she later also had a dream about standing in front of a window with the husband on her right and a new man on her left. It was fine with her husband for her to find a new man. Thus this woman was able to have the security of her love for her husband and also become open to the new.

In his paintings Marc Chagall often used images of brides and bridegrooms. Erich Neumann writes that "in them live the darkness of nocturnal drives and the golden light of the soul's ecstasy."[1] He also states that Chagall is a good example of the soulful and feminine in man. What dominates his pictures is a "configuration of the magical and fascinating, inspiring and ecstatic soul that transforms the world with the starfall of its colors."[2]

If love, beauty, and joy are the rewards at the end of the struggle to unite with the Inner Lover, it doesn't mean that we won't know pain again or that bliss is continuous. It does mean that we are wedded to our inner source of passion and know how to connect with it. We've learned what makes us feel vibrantly alive, aroused, and sensuous. Once we know how to fulfill ourselves that way, it becomes much easier and more fun to relate to other people. We are freer because we don't have to squeeze every drop of love or life out of them. We can enjoy what they give and appreciate them as they are without wishing they'd fulfill something for us. So outer relationships become easier and lighter and more joyful.

One's own life is so much better because the yin-yang, the male-female polarities, have married within oneself They are no longer divorced but in harmony. Happy is the beneficiary of this union. One can draw upon its warm sustenance for a long time.

Just as in an outer marriage, we can daily nurture the bond with our deepest selves. We are happier when we live at the center of our being rather than the fringes. We can escape society's canned prescriptions for life because we have a solid connection to our interior processes.

All this is possible as long as we love our fantasies and follow them like a lover to the ends of the earth. "Whither thou goest, I will go," should be our mantra.

Rage, Grief, and Surrender

Set me as a seal upon thine heart,
as a seal upon thine arm:
for love is strong as death;
jealousy is cruel as the grave:
the coals thereof are coals of fire,
which hath a most vehement flame.

—Song of Solomon 8:6

I n order to attain *voluptas*, we have to *first* move through intense hurt and rage, not just once but again and again. The fire that burns and tortures us is a very creative and transformative fire. It burns parts of us to a crisp and leaves our egos in a desert of white ash so that one surrenders and is open to deep joy. Love's "most vehement flame" needs to be understood carefully.

When we love another, at times we will be disappointed by the outer situation. At first we feel the fire of anger at the other for not doing what we want or living up to our expectation (our image of the beloved). The fire of our hurt or anger will be directed at the relationship itself. ("This is no good.") This fire is on the ego level and feels like hell. In the beginning of this book, I described receiving the image of a fireball of energy, like the sun. This image emerged when I was very angry and lashing out destructively at the other person. The fireball image enabled me to turn from attacking the other person and the relationship toward supporting myself. The fireball image was a constant source of energy available to help me love and create more. This fire is a presence that can be seized. It is renewable. It transcends the plight of the outer situation.

Jean Houston has described the role of wounding in soul work in *The Search for the Beloved*:

> Soulmaking requires that you die to one story to be reborn to a larger one. [The wounding] need not lead to alienation and withdrawal but can lead to the seeding of the world with the newly released powers of the psyche. When psychological energy is no longer bonded to social forms, then, uncensored, depth images and archetypes can have their day.[1]

Wounding cracks the boundaries of what we thought we could bear and yet may contain the seeds of healing and transformation. Letting our wounds stay open allows us to sacrifice the old story to which we were bonded so that the new story may become manifest through us.

Betrayal is the beginning of the journey. Its message is that things are much more than they seem:

> In our betrayal, the other becomes the instrument of God, bringing us to a tragedy that needs our ennoblement in order to understand it. And the only way to be ennobled and to forgive truly is through love. In giving much more than one thought one could, one discovers that one has much more still to give. This is the mystery and miracle of love, and it changes the very fabric of reality, the very structure of our lives. When we are able to *give forth*, to give of ourselves beyond our protective shell and see the other in wonder and astonishment (regardless of how unskilled another's behavior might have been), then something evolutionary happens and we and the betrayal are not the same. Then love is restored, revealing the larger consequence and the deeper unfolding. Thus, for all of its agony and suffering, betrayal is a necessary advance over primal trust, for its challenges and vicissitudes extend the universe, bring love into darkness, and grow the world and ourselves.[2]

Being betrayed or let down by another causes pain precisely to the degree that we love the other. The outcome of betrayal can be fruitful as long as certain dangers are avoided. One is to try to get revenge; unfortunately, this often results in the kind of tragedies that we read about in the newspapers. Another is to deny or devalue the person, to see all the ugly aspects of a person whom one formerly idealized. Another danger is cynicism, a point of view from which one regards love as a cheat or a trap. We complain or whine about the other or our fate. Or, we become paranoid and attempt to prevent treachery by insisting that the other be forever faithful and devoted. Or one can turn the energy against oneself Medea killed her children because her husband betrayed her. Sylvia Plath killed herself. More commonly we sabotage ourselves by devaluing our thoughts and hopes. We decide that passion is too painful and so we avoid it.

If, in time, one reconciles oneself to being hurt, forgiveness is possible. One does not forget or repress or become superpolite to cover up. Rather, one finally reaches a wider context of understanding. The salt of bitterness is changed into the salt of wisdom. But first one must endure the heartache of expansion.

The desire to kill is an immensely creative space as long as one contains and transforms it imaginatively. The desire to kill the beloved, to rage at the gods, and to appease the fires makes one feel like Medusa, with snakes of rage and despair streaming out of one's head. One fears the hurt and rage so much, one tries to contain or push down the vipers—the vituperative voices that hiss at being thwarted. In being pushed down they congeal in one's body and turn it into stone. Then one is numb and unfeeling, hard and aloof. One goes among people with an immovable heart, cold and remote.

If we could obliterate the other, we'd be free, we think. "Let them go," we say, instead of "Let them *be*." We feel guilty and remorseful for having such murderous thoughts. We think there must be something wrong with us.

Instead we could take positive action on behalf of ourselves. As horses kick out their heels, cats bite, dogs snarl, and donkeys bray, we can break through to new territory. In the myths, remember that Athena wore Medusa's head on her shield, showing how anger can be used for protection.

Love finds a way as long as you stay connected to it. When the other has thwarted or rejected you and violence courses through your blood, now is a good time to surrender to kaleidoscopic feelings and await word from the "third player." A supportive and transcendant image, such as mine of the fireball of energy, will come to the rescue.

Containing the rage while awaiting for a supportive image does not mean isolating yourself Part of the process depends on engagement or sharing yourself with the beloved. James Hillman writes, "Reflective insights may arise like the lotus from the still center of the lake of meditation, while creative insights come at the raw and tender edge of confrontation, at the borderlines where we are most sensitive and exposed—and, curiously, most alone."[3] Sometimes we get stuck in the safety of reflecting alone rather than facing up to the new possibilities that can emerge in confronting a loved one. Revealing yourself takes courage.

Let the fires burn until you become empty and transparent, with nothing left to lose. This is like the Japanese saying that when your house burns down, then you can see the moon.

At a point when I was burning up with rage and despair over the relationship with Paul and how he favored Maud, I had a series of dreams in which a fire burned up the interior of my house. In one a female polar bear rose out of the ashes. A polar bear is able to survive extended periods of ice-cold weather, which is what my world felt like then. Her mightiness helped me through that period. Once I dreamed she was carrying me on her back just before I gave birth (and I had not even been sensitive enough to myself to know I was pregnant—the unconscious always prods one into more alertness).

Each time I revealed my true feelings, I also experienced shame. Through the shame, however, I realized that I gained more compassion for myself and others. This is one of the ways life makes us more kindly. Through not hiding, and accepting ourselves totally, we also free others to be more intimate.

Remember, it takes time for suffering to break through the crusts of the heart in order to refine who we are. But, even while this is happening, we are pregnant with new creations. The two processes move together along parallel lines and are dependent on one another.

Therefore, the stages one has to go through before the inner wedding can take place are (1) rage at betrayal or disappointment in the outside person or situation; (2) grief and loneliness occurring simultaneously with rampant fantasies of the Inner Lover; and (3) surrender with gratitude to being rescued by Eros. A joyful marriage then ensues. Soon afterward, the first child will appear in the form of new work, a new sense of self and purpose.

The Creative Offspring

Dream: *I am making a sculpture of a man's head out of dark bronzy clay with many planes or facets. There are large sockets for eyes and full lips. I am screaming with anguish.*

This dream graphically depicts my pain as Eros worked to form a strong principled will within me. The agony comes from having to create out of oneself instead of finding paradise with the outer human. This pain drives you out of apathy and into action. Jung never said that the path of individuation was easy but it is for the best. Through this path you learn to serve your own energy or will instead of someone else's, which allows your soul to engage with the world in a more original way.

It is a paradox that while we reach out ardently for our deepest desires, which are genetically imprinted on our souls, we are also kept from grasping them. But, as we have seen, this is how inner possibilities are opened up. If we didn't desire and reach out, we would never feel the rage of frustration in not getting what we want, or in having to wait for it. "We grow by delays," it has been said. There has to be time for the Inner Lover to open new tributaries for the river of life.

Fantasies and dreams of pregnancy and children often appear to show one's progress. Because creativity is an intensely physical and organic (not just mental) experience, pregnancy and children are symbols for emerging growth. An early pregnancy indicates that a new identity or creative work has come into fruition. A late pregnancy suggests more development. A birthing will probably be accompanied by hard labor as one brings forth a new idea to the outside world. Then, when one dreams of a baby, it is possible that it may be deformed in some way or wants to be fed better food. Best of all, we may be in perfect harmony with the baby.

A woman told me a vivid example of such a dream, which she had soon after her son was born and sleeping on her belly. *He is fucking me under the bed. Our bodies are rolling the pattern of a great mandala. He says, "I'm going to show you tantras you never experienced before." I answer, "But what about my husband?" My son says, "Forget him!"* This dream seems to have rich import for the future.

As a dream child gets older, it will need new forms of care. Dreams in speaking symbolically can be trusted to send messages from the Self to tell us what is needed in our outer existence.

One important child of the inner wedding is the fulfillment of feeling at one with oneself. The archetype of the "sacred prostitute" illustrates this concept.

In ancient times there were temples of the sacred prostitute, where women gave themselves to sex as an act of dedication to the divine powers. Such women were revered for being "at one in themselves." Men were connected to the divine through the conduit of the woman's body. For both, sex was an act of devotion to Eros, as opposed to an individual.

This holy ritual was destroyed when male priests supplanted women in the sacred traditions and declared sex as depraved. Such a mind-body split, which parallels the separation between nature and spirit, has often been cited as the cause of many of our problems. One way we can help heal the world from the devastations of war and alienation is to preserve the connection between sex and spirit or Psyche and Eros. When our souls are integrated, the outer world is brought into harmony as well.

The Joy of Being Mused

> I don't go to her, she comes to me, red
> with unspeakable crimes and her hair
> is a black wind annihilating worlds
>   to get at the door in my bed.
>
> It takes forever to get her clothes off,
>   and I don't have forever.
>
> —Michael Hannon, "The Muse"

The Inner Lover is the muse par excellence. In all the examples given so far in this book, probably the most apparent and delightful result of Inner Lover fantasies is their muse function. To be intensely attracted to another is to be plowed open and freshly fertilized—to be "mused," so to speak. In the relationship between oneself and muse, Erica Jong has stated, it is impossible to tell who is fucking and who is being fucked. As in the above poem, we crave our muses with utmost impatience and cannot control their arrival.

We often think creation means art—painting, poetry, or music. But creation also means forming ideas, making theories, conducting research, raising children, cultivating a garden, nurturing a home, developing a career or business, and planning the next steps in our life. It is also found in our approaches to being with others, our capacity to heal or console, to establish a climate for warmth or closeness, and to act more confidently on behalf of ourselves and our projects.

Our muses are the full gamut of our Inner Lovers: stars, daily partners, friends, brief encounters, any figure who persistently fills our thoughts, dreams, and desires, and leads to creative action. Here are some examples of the Inner Lover as muse.

A businesswoman fell in love with a handsome architect. He was almost twenty years older than she was and had reached a high point in his career. He was recently divorced when he started the affair with the woman, who lived in a tiny city apartment. Much of their time together was spent on weekends at his country retreat in the mountains. The affair did not last long, but her longing for him was great and keen. Because she let herself continue to fantasize and reflect on his qualities, she gradually made some changes. She rented a place in the country for herself, and started a garden, which she'd never done before. She redesigned her apartment, daring to knock out walls to create a more pleasing and original nest for herself The ways in which she changed were more lasting than the relationship itself.

Anaïs Nin tells in her early diaries how she grew up prudish and idealistic. She was a young banker's wife living in Paris when she met Henry and June Miller. Henry was very different from her: his language was vulgar, he lacked decorum, and he was very earthy. June was also very different in that she disguised her past, told lies, and survived by her wits with no source of income. Anaïs was fascinated by her air of mystery and independence and was as obsessed with her as anyone is with a lover.

In her diary she wrote as if to June: "You are the woman I want to be. I see in you that part of me which is you." About Henry: "Henry is dispelling the fogs of shyness, of solitude, taking me through the street, and keeping me in a cafe—until dawn. Before Henry I thought art was the paradise, not human life. . . ."[1]

The result of Anaïs' liaisons with both Henry and June was that she absorbed the qualities she saw in them that were lacking in her. She in a sense took on a new coloration by adding their pigments to her own palette. From Henry she got more deviltry to blend with her idealism. She developed an appreciation for street people, and her writing grew stronger and more direct. From June she cultivated a sense of mystery about her whereabouts and clothes. She became a new woman.

Both of these relationships, which can be followed closely in volume I of *The Diary of Anaïs Nin* and in the film *Henry and June*, were intense episodes, involving much longing, excitement, tension, times of fulfillment, and eventual parting of the ways. As Anaïs tussled with her feelings in the initial stages of attraction and then through the difficulties of involvement, we see her in the process of giving birth to a new self.

One night after a talk with Henry and Larry Durrell, she realized that she would have to go a different way from them, "the woman's way . . . woman's creation far from being like man's must be exactly like her creation of children, that is, it must come out of her own blood, englobed by her womb, nourished with her own milk. It must be a human creation, of flesh, it must be different from man's abstractions."[2]

Finally, her relationship with Henry and June changed from one of obsession to a more distant friendship. It seems as if when the birth of a new self is accomplished, the outer relationships diminish in intensity. You move on to other experiences. Only you can decide whether moving on is an act in accordance with soul growth or whether you are doing it because you refuse to endure the ego suffering of being open to another.

Some Inner Lover musing is specific to creating artistic works. Anne Truitt, a sculptor, describes in her published diary, *Daybook*, how she frequently has a dream about a certain male lover before she does a new piece, as though he impregnates her, and they conceive the idea together. Another artist's creations are sparked by his meditations upon Cezanne's paintings.

In Woody Allen's films we can see how his muse changed, because he so often starred his lovers as characters. Diane Keaton was spunky and light-humored, Mia Farrow more searching and wistful. As Liv Ullman did for Ingmar Bergman, his heroines act out aspects of himself.

In *The Pregnant Virgin*, Jungian analyst Marion Woodman describes a dream that serves another function, that of confirming a woman, Sarah, in her efforts to create, when she feels discouraged.

I am browsing in an old cemetery. The graves are above ground, mostly cement vaults. Suddenly I am aware that the top of one is moving. I stop in amazement about twenty feet from it. The top is being pushed up from underneath. A powerful masculine arm thrusts the top off. An equally powerful hairy leg swings out over the side. A magnificent blond, blue-eyed man rises out of the tomb, laughing and shaking himself Light bounces off his skin. He opens his arms and strides toward me as if I were his long lost love. This is my Dionysian Christ.

Woodman comments:

The masculine spirit freed from the tombs of the world that is now dead for Sarah rises up with the joyous energy of the instinctual masculine and the radiant energy of the spirit. The stone of the past is rolled away and the vibrant new energy moves toward the feminine as if it had loved her all her life, if only she had known how to receive it. . . "He was like the Lord of the Dance," said Sarah. "He made me feel that I was conceived in love. The very cells of my body leapt with love to receive him.".... Such a dream gives a woman tremendous confidence, a confidence she desperately needs if she has betrayed her feeling most of her life.[3]

A married couple described to me how they have been muses for each other in a mutually satisfying partnership. Robert is a music professor, and Diane, his wife, is a classical singer. They perform and teach together. He says about his relationship with her:

It's been enormously important to have someone love me and my way as an artist—with music and piano playing. For her too as a singer it is very important to have someone love her voice, someone who loves her *and* her voice. I have written a number of love songs for her. We have a very complementary relationship. When I was married to this other artist, she made a distinction between respecting me as a composer but despising me as a pianist. This set up a lot of self-doubt in me. But the past ten years with Diane have been so much more comfortable. I am taking risks. For instance, Diane saw I was fascinated with computers and electronic music, and she encouraged me to make big speculative purchases. Also, she read a book of vignettes about mythical beasts, which she thought would be perfect for me to use to stretch my imagination on the synthesizer. I ingested the idea and then I just went for it. Each piece is more outlandish than the one before. It was the nth degree in imaginative play in sound. Incredible challenges. I also had her voice in mind as I created it. We already have a commitment for a concert. Her encouragement has been so important.

Diane adds:

I'm attracted to the way Robert keeps his finances, the way he relates to humans beings, the way he enjoys his solitude, the way he eats his breakfast. I just think he is infinitely fascinating. He is totally absorbed in everything he does. We love our work. We help each other in everything we do. We go over our datebooks together and schedule. Our lives are intertwined twenty-four hours a day. We also have a financial ritual. We have our separate accounts and joint accounts. We pay each other and yet spontaneously treat each other. Money becomes this really fun thing we play with. We encourage each other to spend or charge more. We have a whole lot of spontaneous synergy now.

They both said that they would not have been able to achieve this creative musing without having learned through previous mistakes in relationships how to do it better.

While they achieved musing through closeness, others need distance. For instance, many people cultivate attachments to people in prison, pen pals, those long dead. These faraway others act as muses for these people, who evoke their creativity through outpourings in letters. For instance, in the cartoon about Brenda Starr, ace reporter, there was always a "mystery man," whom she loved more than any other man but rarely saw. We often observe how artists prefer to spend long hours with their muses rather than other people, even though they bewail their loneliness.

The muse in facilitating creation requires freedom from constraints. When we are warm and respectful toward our Inner Lovers, they flow better than when we try to use them to further our ego desires for fame or money. Norman Mailer once wrote about how fickle the "bitch goddess success" is. Muses have their own rhythm and timing and will not be pushed around. Most so-called creative blocks have to do with not respecting the deep voice of the muse enough. We can rail against our Inner Lovers or muses and call them names for not appearing when we want them to, but they will not be harnessed. They are free agents. That's why it's smart to drop everything when they come calling.

Inner Lovers as muses trash old ideas in favor of the new and more complex. But for one to muse the most original contributions to a culture requires surrendering to the deepest experiences Inner Lovers exert. Jung wrote, "Only the passionate yearning of a highly developed mind . . . can create a new symbol. But inasmuch as the symbol proceeds from his highest and latest mental achievement and must also include the deepest roots of his being, it cannot be a one-sided product of the most highly differentiated mental functions, but must at least have an equal source in the lowest and most primitive motions of his psyche."[4] Deep, concentrated reflection may be arduous to sustain but from it have come profound and satisfying works.

There are many sublime examples of those whose Inner Lovers have become muses. John Milton's *Paradise Lost* contains images written out of the despair he felt when his first wife temporarily left him. William Butler Yeats' love for Maud Gonne inspired some of his best poems. T. S. Eliot had a long friendship with Emily Hale, about whom a reviewer wrote, "If Eliot was ever in love with Emily Hale, it was in some ethereal and spectral sense, a love beyond desire. . . . He kept Emily hanging about, full of expectation, as if she had nothing better to do than maintain his symbolism."[5]

A therapist writes about Dante's *Divine Comedy:*

> Dante's fleeting vision of the fourteen-year-old Beatrice was sufficient to inspire him to travel the long and painful way to paradise. Instead of bewailing the fact that he could not love her in earthly terms, he allowed the love her image awoke in his soul to take him to the psychological place wherein he could unite with "her" for eternity. By treasuring his love for her, he allowed himself to meet and suffer all those qualities within himself which blocked or obscured a union with his image of the supreme beauty, grace, and purity of the feminine. He did not allow anger, frustration, denial, or even the numbness of passing time to dim the image of his love, but let it flourish within his soul until it became his soul.[6]

Some psyches depend on Eros. Richard Wagner wrote about his feminine side as essential to his ability to create. He needed to be ardent, to focus on a beloved in the act of poetic and musical composition. He said, "Women are very much the music of life." George Balanchine, the choreographer, echoed that sentiment when he said that all his dances were conceived by seeing female muses dancing in his head. One of his dancer-muses, Suzanne Farrell, has recently written a memoir. She was eighteen, he fifty-nine when they met. He was violently in love with her, but although they interacted frequently, they never discussed more of a relationship. When she married another, though, he reacted like a betrayed lover, banishing her from the troupe and working out his anguish in new creations. The artistic purpose to their connection overwhelmed any personal satisfaction.

Truly, one of the most intricate Inner Lover musings ever to take place was that of Plato and Socrates. Plato was devoted to praising the wisdom of Socrates, who inspired him. But, interestingly, it is Plato we come to know more, because it is his mind that created the books through which we experience Socrates.

Spirit Blossoms

A special word needs to be said about deliberately devoting oneself to the Inner Lover more than the outer. As I stated at the beginning, it is by no means the aim of this book to encourage people to live in the realm of fantasy and to avoid human bonds. The problem with most of us is that we look too much to others for gratification that they cannot provide, while we miss the rich depth of our own beings. Thus, this book can be seen as an attempt to point out and help correct an imbalance. With more discriminating inner awareness, outer relationships are more peaceful. As you take responsibility for your own passion, you can actually enjoy the nourishment you receive from others more.

But there are certain people for whom the inner life is already very important. The vast literature of psychology and spirituality affirms their experiences. Many of these people have found the treasures of solitude and bring the gifts of their spirit to the people with whom they come in contact. They earnestly desire to become transparent to the Divine Will and to be used as its instrument in this world.

Celibates who dedicate themselves to the Beloved (as an image of God) are an example. We know how similar some of their writings are to the ecstasies of love. These *religieux* know clearly that their consummations are spiritual. They do not address a real person. They address God or Jesus or the Dark One or Allah as their Inner Lover.

Here is a song by Mirabai, "Why Mira Can't Go Back to Her Old House," translated by Robert Bly. (Mirabai was a princess and mystic in sixteenth-century India who renounced the world out of her great love for Lord Krishna.)

The colors of the Dark One have penetrated Mira's body; all the other colors washed out.

Making love with the Dark One and eating little, those are my pearls and my carnelians.

Meditation beads and the forehead streak, those are my scarves and my rings.

That's enough feminine wiles for me. My teacher taught me this.

Approve me or disapprove me: I praise the Mountain Energy night and day.

I take the path that ecstatic human beings have taken for centuries.

I don't steal money, I don't hit anyone. What will you charge me with?

I have felt the swaying of the elephant's shoulders; and now you want me to climb on a jackass?

Try to be serious!

In a discussion about celibacy and her community, a nun said: "Mysticism is not disguised sex; sex is disguised mysticism." The deepest hunger in every person is the hunger for God. People find it through love and sex. People can choose not to follow their sex desire. "Here we do not settle down with one particular person; we are called to love all. . . . The whole world becomes friends and spouse. That is a tremendous challenge, and has great rewards."

In *The Art of Sexual Ecstasy*, Margo Anand writes about the Tantric tradition, in which devotees are encouraged to visualize in great detail the form and qualities of a divine lover, such as the god Shiva or the goddess Shakti. Their aim is to focus with such devotion on the spiritual beloved that they ultimately attain union with the deity, thereby manifesting in themselves the divine qualities of the godhead."[1]

The ideals of love, truth, and beauty are found within ourselves. Dialogues and prayers throughout history have oriented our longing in this direction. Jean Houston, in *The Search for the Beloved*, elaborates on this theme: "In all the great spiritual and mystery traditions, the central theme, the guiding passion, is the deep yearning for the Beloved of the soul." The yearning is a memory of a spiritual union that goes very deep and fails to go away, "a union that is only partially explained and mirrored through human loving or partnership."[2]

In the mystery of love, as one learns to love another truly, one finds the Divine Lover revealed within that other human being. Then, like a Mother Teresa, one cannot do enough for the other, for it is done for the Beloved. One looks at the other with the eyes of the Beloved when one is able to see him or her in wonder and astonishment, in the fullness of human glory, even amid the conditions of everyday life. This "double vision" empowers and releases the other to become who he or she truly is. This is the "look of love."

The life and work of the Sufi mystic Jelaluddin Rumi are a powerful example of love and the flowers of spirit. Born in 1207 in what is now Afghanistan, he later settled in Anatolia. He was trained in traditional theology and became a distinguished professor. When he was around forty, a wild dervish and wanderer named Shams-i-Tabriz appeared and threw Rumi's books into the water, saying, "Now you must live what you know." They fell into love, leaving their past ways of life. Rumi's students were jealous and upset and drove Shams away after one hundred and one days. Rumi poured his heartbreak into poetry and dance, meanwhile sending his son to search for Shams. Shams was found and brought back, but after months of ecstatic reunion with Rumi, was murdered by the students. Inside Rumi burned and burned, ultimately producing thousands of poems that have been cherished for centuries.

His poems dramatize the Inner Lover journey. Rumi perceived the divine image and message beyond the person of Shams. He transformed his love for the actual man into illuminating poems. Here is a version of a poem, called "The Naked Sun," that speaks of spiritual pregnancy:

> Those who live in Union
> become pregnant with the feelings and words
> of invisible forms!
> > Their amazed mouths
> open. Their eyes withdraw.
>
> Children are born of that illumination.
> We say "born," but that's not right.
> It only points to a new understanding.
>
> Be quiet and let the Master of Speech talk.
> Don't try to dress up your own nightingale-song
> to sell to this Rose! Be all ear.
> This pregnancy!
> > So subtle and delicious,
> the way ice in July reminds us of winter,
> the way fruit in January tells of summer
> generosity,
> > that's how the naked Sun
> embraces all the orchard-brides at once.[3]

The last two lines recall how in India artworks show Krishna with many women at once. He is in effect the Inner Lover for many women. One could also say that Krishna himself has many Inner Lovers as represented by the women.

While self-proclaimed mystics may be charged with energy that they express as longing for God to fill their hearts, their words are just a different spin on being open to the interior Self. They speak of the divine way. However, the sacred manifests in many ways, and to see it does not require a religious vocabulary.

A *religieux* may concentrate more on God than the world (though not necessarily), while another person may be focused more on business than Self. The only danger for either is to ignore the wisdom of their bodies through denial, detachment, abstraction, or hurry. Rumi was a holy man who did not. Much to the consternation of his religious followers, he persisted in his love for Shams. His poems embrace physical feelings and instruct us about their sacred numinosity.

A Gift to Oneself and the World

The fusion of Inner Lovers within our psyches brings gifts of new ideas not only to ourselves but also to the world. Another gift we can give to the world when we have reached this state is greater harmony. When you are not blaming another but allowing yourself to burn creatively and passionately, you create a climate of openness with others that promotes respect and truth.

The world needs people who are operating on all their cylinders to save it from destruction. Jean Houston says, "The world may be urging us to coalesce into a new and higher unity for which we feel unprepared, and the only force emotionally powerful enough to call us to educate ourselves for sacred stewardship is communion and partnership with the Beloved."[1] Thus, when we unite with our Inner Lovers, our capacities for greater thinking, feeling, sensing, and learning are expanded; consequently our relationships with others and the world are vastly improved. The message is loud and clear that the expansion of consciousness resulting from the communion between Psyche and Eros matters greatly.

In his book *The Universe Is a Green Dragon*, physicist Brian Swimme uses the language of Eros as a metaphor for the magnetism in the universe.

> By pursuing your allurements, you help bind the universe
> together. The unity of the world rests on the pursuit of passion. . . .
> Bring to mind all the allurements filling the universe, of whatever
> complexity or order: the allurement we call gravitation, that of
> electromagnetic interactions, chemical attractors, allurements in
> the biological and human worlds. . . . [If these are blocked, we
> see] galaxies, human families, atoms, ecosystems, all disintegrat-
> ing immediately as the allurement pervading the universe is shut
> off. Nothing left. No community of any sort.[2]

Atoms search for union to form molecules. Molecules in resonance form more complex systems, the connective energy being the
lure that brings about the next steps in evolution. In this way new
associations, genes, and forms are created. In using the language of
quantum physics, humans are both wave and particle, in the composition of their bodies and the relational capacities of their minds.[3]

Furthermore, the genes of our body-mind (psyches) are constantly being renewed and responding to our habitats (including
other people). Quantum physics and the theory of relativity have
shown that consciousness has a great deal to do with the results.
In *Space, Time, and Medicine* Larry Dossey states, "The new view
of consciousness asserts unabashedly that conscious mental activity exerts measurable effects on the physical world—a world that
includes human bodies, organs, tissues, and cells."[4]

Since our consciousness is shaped so extensively by the penetration of our psyches with Eros, let us look more closely at how
the energy of love flows from us to impact the world.

Biology, Psyche, and Destiny

What is the nature of the bond between psyche and world? In
physical terms, the human psyche originates from the same chemical substances as the earth's matter. We share the same atoms
as stars. Genes perpetuate themselves. The DNA code found in
humans has been shaped by history and culture, although it has
been hard to measure the extent of their influences. Biologists
locate ethics and the activity of the unconscious in the limbic
center of the brain. Some scientists, such as the noted biologist

E. O. Wilson, believe that it is not precisely known how the wiring of the brain's neurons, which is encoded in the genes, influences behavior.[5]

But the major psychologists to date, Sigmund Freud and C. G. Jung, both trained as scientists, theorized in different ways about the relationship between human biology and behavior. Freud's theories centered on behavior related to the mouth, anus, and genitals. For him the unconscious was primarily the locus of repressed sexual and aggressive instincts. Jung regarded the instincts as channels for reflection, creativity, and activity. He viewed the unconscious not only as personal but also collective in that it contained a storehouse of cultural symbols, from which a unique identity was formed. Jung, possibly to counteract Freud's authority, stressed the spiritual attributes of the motivating drives.

Psychology is a landmark science in that it is a science of subjectivity, complete with characteristics, cycles, and structure. (Einstein's relativity theory has contributed to our understanding that it is entirely possible that there is no such thing as "objective reality" at all, separate from human perception of it.) In the present time when machines duplicate and manipulate genetic codes, it is probably more essential than ever to understand the purpose and value of subjectivity. Love is its very core.

Jonathan Lear explicates Freud's view in *Love and Its Place in Nature*:

> The process by which the human soul comes to be is a lifetime activity. Love, Freud said, tends toward ever higher unities . . . [It] fuels a dialectic of development. . . . As I develop in complexity, so does the world as it exists for me. The internalization of structure can thus continue at ever higher levels of complexity and refinement.[6]

To the argument that psychoanalysis is not an objective science but almost a matter of faith like religion, he states:

> Of course, there *is* a serious question as to how one tests, adjusts or legitimates psychoanalytical theory, given that the criteria of

evaluation are, broadly speaking, internal. How does one criticize, alter or even undermine a theory from the inside? Simply to
dismiss psychoanalysis as a "matter of faith" is to ignore this question. It is to assume that an objective science must be evaluable
from the outside . . .[7]

He then goes on to argue that psychoanalysis should not have
to fit into a pre-existing concept of "science," when the definition
of science itself might not be good enough.

Pursuing the importance of subjectivity and its principles of
operation, Ira Progoff posited an "evocative science," calling his
particular spin on it holistic depth psychology.[8] The technique he
developed to enable people to both activate and find meaning in
all the threads and energies of their lives was the Intensive Journal method. I want to highlight two of his terms—process and
holism—to illustrate more about how destiny emerges out of the
dialectics of biology and psyche.

Process refers to the continuity we observe in the world—from
the chemistry, biology, and physics of evolution to the history of
civilizations. It also includes the variety of inner experiences we
have. *Holism* refers to the fact that "evolutionary processes bring
about ever more refined holistic units, new forms of life, new spe-
cies, coming into existence by virtue of the inherently integra-
tive process in evolution. These holistic units are entirely new
and unpredictable emergents."[9] They constitute the way in which
creative possibilities are brought into the world. Thus, within us
new integrations form spontaneously out of the process of our
experiences, and these not only affect our individual lives but
enter the atmosphere of the world.

Progoff believes that subjective process is "so distinct a realm of
experience and observation with its inherent principles and phe-
nomenology that it deserves the attention that would be given to
a full field of study." The features that distinguish human experience from conventional views of science are "the consciousness
of self, the tangible effects of subjective feelings and judgments,
the degrees of freedom in thought and action, the possibilities of
individual creativity."[10]

Within subjective process, cycles can be observed, which I briefly generalize here. In nature when a creature dies, it is recycled into the earth's chemical substances. When a human thought, idea, or project breaks up and comes to an end, it does not disintegrate but goes into our memory bank with the wishes, images, thoughts, and emotions connected to it. "They are on reserve, waiting for a new situation to arise where they can be combined with other factors and resume their active life in a new context."[11] *Process* can be said to be continuous and inclusive of constructive and destructive elements. Its cycles move between opposite stages (what we call highs and lows, dark and light, love and hate) and take on a life of their own with beginning, middle, and end. They give rise to new integrations and holistic units, as mentioned above.

Progoff developed the structure of the Intensive Journal to facilitate the optimum conditions for creative "emergents" to occur. Obviously, the purpose and value of these emergents go beyond the destiny of the individual. They add to our understanding of the realities and meaning of life and contribute to the destiny of the world.

Knowing this, we may appreciate more the personal and universal benefits of developing close communion with our psyches. The psyche is the source of all human activities. No house was ever built, no work of art or scientific discovery ever made without the participation of the human psyche. Anything that applies to the psyche applies to all of human existence, and thus understanding the dynamics of the unconscious is crucial. If, for instance, we could just realize how we as individuals and nations project evil onto others, we would gain in our ability to deal with it more insightfully.

Intercourse with Inner Lovers will sensitize us more to the agonies of illness and war in the world, because our beings are expanded and refined. With aware psyches, we become more capable of clear, compassionate, and just action. Thus, having the knowledge imbedded in the tissues of our beings that longing leads to joyful union and wisdom can be enormously helpful to others in the world.

In the beginning of this book, I discussed Teilhard de Chardin's comment that if we could harness the energy of love, we could change the world. To harness this energy requires bringing Psyche and Eros together. Our personal Inner Lovers will start a ripple in our selves that will ultimately expand into much larger truths.

PART FIVE

How to Use Inner Lover Fantasies

Working with Dreams and Images

Because Inner Lovers reveal deep truths and meaning in our lives, we need ways of connecting with them in ongoing, dependable ways. Dreams and images and inner dialoguing can bring us to the illuminations and intimations that await us in the depths of our beings.

Just cultivating an attitude of friendly receptivity to the unconscious in the form of fantasies, images, and dreams enlarges your life immensely. Anyone who does not do this is missing half of life. Working with a therapist who is attuned to *evoking* the depth material as opposed to analyzing it is a journey that can benefit you and ultimately the larger community around you. I also recommend learning ways of becoming attuned to the non-verbal unconscious messages coming from your body. For example, working with chakras, tensions in muscles, postural adaptations, and energy responses to others can help sensitize you to the Lover within and treat it as an honored guest in your heart.

I agree with Jean Houston, who writes in *The Search for the Beloved*: "To deepen the relationship with the Beloved (a soul image), follow the same principles of relationship that you pursue in the human realm. Thus, you live the relationship throughout the day, bringing the same sensitivity to nuance and fine tuning that you would bring to a human love relationship."[1] This could include special greetings, ritual gestures, altars, and gifts. Together live through the day in partnership with your Inner Lover, solving problems and enjoying pleasures.

Practicing your connection to the Inner Lover faithfully can increase your capacity to live in two worlds and offers great freedom and capacity to love. It helps to have an actual creative work in progress, for a critical intention of the Inner Lover is to become a creative force in the universe, not just in the ordinary self. In this way our love forges reality.

Meditating on the mystery and meaning of the Inner Lover is a good place to start practicing your connection. This meditation doesn't have to be any highly disciplined focus on an esoteric mantra. It can be simply setting aside at least fifteen minutes one or two times a day to sit or lie quietly with your eyes closed. At first your mind may just be a blank. It will need some quieting down and detaching from your previous activities. It is best not to guide or direct your thoughts in any way because doing so interferes with the spontaneous and more authentic messages from the Self. If you try to picture yourself lying in a meadow by a waterfall with a lover, you are imposing a wish upon the screen, which is of little use. Better to observe the thoughts, feelings, and pictures that come of their own accord.

June Singer believes that many forms of meditation are designed to liberate the energies that have been blocked and bring them into a universal context. She writes, "Meditation is a way of tending the fire, of keeping alive and active the process of conscious evolution."[2] At times meditation eliminates the separation between subject and observer. Then we are open to mutual penetration.

Imaging

The images that come up are not just visual pictures. They can be thoughts, feelings, sounds, or hunger signals—in short, whatever appears during the interval you have relaxed your mind. The quantity of images doesn't matter at all. Some people see nothing for long periods; others may be bombarded with images, which, when examined, tend to be saying the same thing but in a hundred different ways. The important point is to be aware of the images, perhaps write them down, and reflect on them, as if turning over stones in your palm.

Often images come not in meditations but unexpectedly while walking or driving a car or any other time when your mind is free. For many people fruitful times are before sleeping at night or just on waking in the morning. At those moments you are in a twilight level, between waking and sleeping, and your conscious mind is more open to the stream of activity coming from the unconscious. Actually this stream is always flowing below the surface of our activities. All it takes is quieting down to take a peek at what is going on there.

This stream carries intuitions, insights, symbols, perceptions of truth and meaning, and ideas that synthesize information in surprising ways. Its style is more metaphoric and allusive than direct and literal, even though this is the level that produces sensations of discovery ("ah ha!") or peaceful centering. When we have fantasies about our Inner Lovers, we are usually conducted along this stream. That is why our Inner Lovers are considered bridges to the unconscious or deeper Self. They are persons who help us make deep connections.

So it is important to let your impulses to fantasize flow. Have one thousand and one, have two thousand and one fantasies, as long as they naturally last. For your Inner Lovers can guide you to important knowledge about the conduct of your life and ultimately your purpose in the world, if you surrender to them. That means living with them and letting their meaning unfold inside you.

If you let yourself dwell on and play with your images, you will surely realize what qualities in the outer person and situation so attract you. Every time you fantasize you take in a little more soul food, though thinking of a person as a rich source of nourishment can be an excruciating paradox when you are feeling severely deprived, as though the goodies are being withheld from you. However, inside many of us exists a great emptiness, which the Inner Lover fills.

When we have lived enough years, we have a number of Inner Lovers operating purposefully within us. We can sit down at the round table with them and see what they have to say. Remember to call upon your Inner Lovers deliberately to come to your aid when you are in difficult situations. Think how would this person face the problem you have; then access that power. When we use our Inner Lovers, their qualities infuse our way of being on a daily basis.

It's especially important not to run away from the images when you are upset by how much you long for the other or by how tumultuous you feel. Sometimes we are desperate to leap out of the fire, but cutting ourselves off tends to block our connection with deeper sources of knowledge and love. It makes us harder and drier and ultimately emptier. It is better to really dive into the desires, letting their eroticism enflame you. Longing fuels your imagination. At the same time, a splendid center is forged within you that is bright, passionate, and independent. Paradoxically, being defenseless to love will make you stronger than ever. You surrender or melt into that which is greater than yourself.

Dreams

You may sometimes wonder if it all isn't too much, especially if the outer person is not responding in the desired way (which is usually the case!). This is where dreams can guide you. Dreams are objective and impersonal statements from the psyche. Through them destiny whispers to us. They orient us to what is beautiful as well as to what is cruel. Dreams are to be trusted. They absolutely will not fail to respond to our situations, especially if we are in turmoil.

Freud called dreams "the royal road to the unconscious." It is also said that a dream ignored is like an unopened letter from the Self. Who wants to ignore such messages? Ira Progoff describes how dreams carry the "seed-nature" of a person. They "express the outward circumstances of a person's life, his current problems and fears, and also the hopes and goals toward which he is consciously planning. In addition, however, dreams reflect the deeper-than-conscious goals that are seeking to unfold in a person's life. These may be the long-range purposes that set the fundamental directives of a life, and yet are not consciously known by the person himself"[3] So it is well worthwhile to do whatever you can to weave dreams into the fabric of your life.

Jung wrote, "As a plant produces its flower, so the psyche creates its symbols. Thus, through dreams, intuitions, impulses, and other spontaneous happenings, instinctive forces influence the activity of consciousness."[4]

In *The Symbolic Life* he also states that people have lost connection with the numinosity of life, and dreams give it back. The unconscious makes you realize that there's been a gap in your memory. The emotionality of dreams is their point. "Dreams seem to consider it their main task to bring back a sort of recollection of the prehistoric as well as the infantile world, right down to the level of the most primitive instincts, as if such memories were a priceless treasure."[5]

Jung stressed the importance of not trying to figure everything out and accepting what happens, good and bad. In other words, in accepting God's will, life becomes more exciting and deeply satisfying.

Depth psychologists trust that the Self is working something out regardless of the individual. The Self has a life of its own, which, nevertheless, must be experienced in the body and brought into the world. The insights brought out of the dark unconscious to the light of consciousness do not only take place in your mind, they actually change the structure of your physical cells, as holistic health experts and mind-body-spirit therapists have noted. Just as a drop of something will totally change a chemical solution, so a bit of conscious realization affects us.

When we dream about a Lover, we need to see that Lover as a part of ourselves. We need to ask how we think, act, or feel as that person. I am frequently asked, "How do you know whether the dream is about the outer person or about the Inner Lover?" This can be answered in a variety of ways. You can assume that dreams are both about yourself and about others. Or, to put it another way, they are about the outer situation but with a deeper message for yourself. Ultimately, the inner and outer are one and the same, with no distinctions between the two realms.

The fact is that when we are strongly attracted to someone, we are responding to qualities we see in the person, and our dreams will partially be about the relationship between us. But our attraction and our dreams are directing us far beyond the person. It is as though the other person is a small circle and the circumference of our dream potential a much wider one. The other person is too small a subject for all that is being implied by a dream. Thus, you need to take a wider view.

Dreams use figures from our personal lives to tell us something we need to know about ourselves. Thus, men and women who were important to us in the past may appear in the present. Often these figures will appear in different guises to make a point. A man, beardless in actuality, may have bushy eyebrows and a thick beard, which shows that in you he has become more pronounced, perhaps shady. A thin person may appear very bloated. He or she may have a rash or behave coldly. It is not at all uncommon for a figure to become more peaceful and gentle over time, which both reflects and facilitates a shift in your attitude toward yourself.

Sometimes to remind yourself of the more than personal nature of a dream figure, it can help to slightly alter the person's name. For instance, you could call a Carl "Carlo," a Jane "Janey."

In dreams you may also find yourself making love with unfamiliar figures. Dialogue with them and find out who they are and what they want to give you. Some new dimension or idea is pressing to be added to your life.

Here is a dream by a woman who was feeling stuck and incapable in her life. *I am trying to ski up a hill but my knees hurt and are crippled, unable to move me. A young man, handsome and decked out in ski apparel, skis up to me and offers to help. My shoes/boots also won't stay on the skis well. He pushes me up the hill and says, "Is that enough?" I let him know I want more. He is leaning over me and smells of sweet cologne. Then he lets me go on my own and I ski downhill fairly well.* In this example a completely unknown man appeared out of the unconscious to aid her by giving her the support she needed.

In thinking about your dreams it's a good idea not to get hung up on the interpretation of symbols. Images have different meanings dependent on the associations of the dreamer. As you pay more attention to your dreams, you will notice what themes reappear. Your dreams use your own experiences and cultural context to instruct you. Thus, you'll want to come to your own personal interpretation of the meaning in the images.

Since dreams often present you with details and situations from the past that will be relevant for your present conundrum, it's useful to describe at length what was going on at the time referred to. See if in doing so a shock of awareness doesn't come over you to help you in your current situation.

Animal and Mythical Motifs

The individual psyche will also reveal itself through archetypal motifs, represented by mythological figures and animals. Archetypes are the cultural symbols that are common to us all, yet we each experience them in our own personal way. Examples are the sun, moon, earth, Mother, Father, Child, initiations, sacrifices, transformation, birth, death, journey, home, demons, trees, roses, gardens, lakes, rivers, mountains, deserts, and so forth. There are also more mundane motifs such as cities, schools, dentists, and doctors.

Out of the innumerable myths, the only ones that have power are those that emerge organically out of the context of your own life. The psyche dramatizes its needs through symbolic forms and stories, or myths. It seeks to enlarge the scope of our lives to fulfill purposes that are keyed into our genetic code. The symbolic layers of the psyche exist beyond consciousness, beyond the intellect, and beyond control. We apprehend their meaning as our lives (stories) unfold.

Through most of this book I have focused on the images of men and women as Inner Lovers, but they can also be represented by images of animals and mythical creatures, such as eagles, owls, great fish, lions, tigers, bears, monkeys, cats, dogs, snakes, gods and goddesses from cultures all over the world. The more understanding we have of these images, the more their energies can flow into us. You can use the Inner Wisdom dialogue, described below, to help you comprehend their meaning for you.

For me the horse has been a major figure, often showing me how aligned I have or have not been with my deepest goals. When I am in danger of burnout, it will appear tired, haggard, and neglected. It has often wanted me to give it a looser rein. In fact, it has wanted me to drop the reins altogether and just go along for the ride, which is hard to do. Over time it has come to embody my power, beauty, and passion.

A woman had a series of dreams over the years about monkeys. The first time one appeared, it was small and sat on her desk. The dream told her that the monkey (hence, she too) had to be broken apart, with its guts spilling out, in order to grow. After a long period during which she courageously broke away from a cruel man, she then dreamed of a very large, human-size monkey, who lay on a funeral pyre saying, "Thy will be done." The framework of these dreams concerned all that was necessary in transformation. She associated monkeys with evolution. In her view her personal evolution involved having to spill her guts, give her all, and surrender to the Divine Will.

Often both men and women encounter a wild, shaggy, feral creature, who calls upon them to leave their conventional and domesticated lives and to integrate more animal instinctuality. Dreams will show the transformative stages of ancient rituals, in which the selected initiates are beaten into surrendering the past and laid asunder for the new dynamism to enter. When such powerful images appear, it can be very helpful to research the myth or animal so that you can study and incorporate (literally take into your body) its elements.

Writing a dream down exactly as you remember it is the first step. Then you can be creative about expanding your associations on dream images. You can draw pictures of dreams or more abstract responses to the feeling tone. You can write a dream out like a free-verse poem, with slashes between the main phrases. You can make a story out of it.

One point to keep in mind is that one dream is not the whole story. For a fuller story you want to look at a series of dreams over time. Eventually the complete story comes after we have lived our whole lives. Each dream is an aspect of it.

It's important to look at dreams in series because dreams tend to be corrective mechanisms to our daily thoughts and actions. If we are veering too far to the right, the wind of the unconscious steers our boat to the left. Getting a sense of the direction, finding out which way the wind is blowing, is the objective.

Telling a dream to a friend, a therapist, or a tape recorder is enormously helpful. Hearing yourself loosens your thoughts and feelings and makes you more receptive to a dream's meaning.

Use journals, music, dance, rituals, or prayer to call forth your Inner Lovers. These are ways to mediate between the issues behind what is happening to you and what you are feeling about them.

Ask yourself, what is the correlation between what is happening in my life and the dream story? Sometimes the dream or image will lead you into the future. Other times it might seem to be a direct contradiction of the path you are on. The dream invariably points out something that you are not aware of. Take an active role in finding out what the dream is saying. Don't just be a helpless witness.

The gestalt technique of working with dreams, developed by Fritz Perls, involves treating each object in the dream as a part of oneself and asking it to speak to you. Here is an excerpt from a woman's journal that shows how she addressed such images. The first line of her dream was: *I am with a female companion, both of us dressed in lovely, long flower-print dresses, walking on a blacktop path in the woods. . . .*

ME: Female Companion, who are you and what are you doing in my dream?

FEMALE COMPANION: I am those resources within you that will always be there, that you can always rely on. I accompany you wherever you go.

Me: Silk Dresses, who are you and what are you doing in my dream?

Silk Dresses: We are those "feminine" fetters, those clinging stereotypes in your mind that trip you up. We keep you from moving freely.

Me: Footpath, who are you and what are you doing in my dream?

Footpath: I am the road that you follow when you adapt and conform. I am necessary, and I will take you to prescribed destinations. But to follow me slavishly is to miss a great deal.[6]

Active Imagination

One way to work with dreams or images, other than passively observing them, is to enter into them again as a participator—an approach Jung called "active imagination."

The idea behind active imagination is that the human ego is a balancing point between the conscious and unconscious. On the one hand, too much weight should not be given the unconscious; this is what has usually happened to so-called psychotics, who are at the mercy of unconscious voices. They may have prophetic insights but have lost the ability to channel them into the essentials of living, the need to eat, sleep, and work. On the other hand, most of us are too far over on the conscious side, always concerned with acquiring social wealth and power and not concerned enough with the evolutionary symbols arising in our souls. So the ego works best when it can interact with the unconscious, which is often seen as analogous with fate or God's will. Mediating between our personal needs and the impersonal goals of the unconscious is both an opportunity and responsibility to participate in the cocreation of our lives. For the unconscious depends on us to carry out its aims, and we are dependent on it for its strength and wisdom.

Robert Johnson writes in *Inner Work*, "The two levels of consciousness flow into each other in the field of imagination like two rivers that merge to form one powerful stream. The dialogue of conscious mind with unconscious gives rise to the transcendent function, the Self, that stands as the synthesis of the two."[7]

The Self can be trusted to send you an image that will transcend the conflict between the conscious and unconscious.

In reentering your dreams or fantasies, you contribute your own information and values and viewpoint; your ego talks to, befriends, and argues with persons in the inner world. Inner figures have no final authority over the ego; the ego plays a balancing role. Thus, you don't need to push toward a desired conclusion. Active imagination enables us to debate everyday conflicts, live out unlived parts of ourself, and enhance the search for meaning in our lives.

The onset of a relationship usually produces a dream from the unconscious that signals the theme. An example of this is the dream I had after my first dinner with Paul, in which we were eating from a bowl of insects covered with purple syrup. I connected insects with unusually sensitive communication and purple syrup with the coating of passion. In actuality much of our subsequent time was spent talking erotically.

During a relationship, of course, many dreams and images will comment on the state of what is happening. Dreams will certainly indicate when damage is being done and when certain words or actions should be avoided. After a relationship ends, dreams will often send clarifying messages. For instance, after my husband and I parted, I dreamed of horses covered with mange, which indicated how severely I had neglected myself and been neglected.

The images will show in no uncertain terms when you are clinging to an empty relationship or neglecting yourself in some destructive way. For instance, a woman dreamed about a man she'd been dating. The dream showed that he had blood poisoning; consequently she did not further the relationship. The images will also show where a relationship is alive, needing attention, and hence still capable of transforming you.

Dreaming of copulation is common to us all. The unconscious can send up dreams and images that are much more sexually fantastic than our conscious mind can conceive. Sex is not only a primary instinct but also a metaphor for union of enormous variety. It's no accident that even the most religious people use erotic language to express their deepest intuitions and ecstasies.

Thus, it's crucial not to be squeamish about the sexuality of your dreams but to pay close attention to the details and tone of what's happening.

Jeremy Taylor writes in *Dream Work* that "a more conscious and less repressed attitude toward ourselves as sexual beings is absolutely necessary for our collective survival. . . . [E]rotic desire itself can become a meditative means to increasing wholeness, deepened spiritual experience, and vital human reconciliation."[8]

A practical way to work with your dreams then is to keep a chronological record of your dreams separate from any elaborations of them. That way you can always go back to them and consider them in their "pure" state. Over time new thoughts will come to you. Also, instead of analyzing them, let yourself reenter them and see where they lead. Get comfortable, close your eyes, and put yourself back into the atmosphere and feeling of the dream, just as if you were injecting yourself into a story. For dreams are pieces of a very large story, the end of which you cannot know. But you can glimpse their complexities by immersing yourself in them and letting revelations unfold in their own timing.

And finally, be sure to act on the wisdom gleaned. Jung writes: "The images of the unconscious place a great responsibility upon a man. Failure to understand them, or a shirking of ethical responsibility, deprives him of his wholeness and imposes a painful fragmentariness on his life."[9]

Inner Dialoguing

Regarding states of love, you will no doubt have to remind yourself again and again to resist the tendency to criticize your lover or blame fate. When the intensity or anguish heats up, it's essential not to let the person *go* but to *be*. On the one hand, we need to base the outer relationship on reality. On the other, we need to see what the unconscious is trying to communicate through the person and the relationship. Here is where the technique of dialoguing is useful.

Although we all dream, some people do not try to keep track of their dreams. To Ira Progoff that is not a problem. He thinks that dialogues can be as valuable as dreams in terms of accessing deep material from the unconscious. With the same capacity for activating potentials and deep insights, dialogues have the additional asset of being easier to understand than dreams.

The technique of dialoguing is a highly valuable discipline in coming to appreciate the Self of a cherished other. Most of the time we are centered on our own perceptions. We may know intellectually that every person sees the world uniquely but we all too often get furious or upset with another for being different from us. Through this kind of friction we gain a necessary and beneficient understanding of the other. Some call this "space between" sacred because each person carries a piece of the Divine, and when we explore this space, we are coming closer to It. At any rate, when we truly love another, the binds we get into with that person will open us to universal truths. The method of dialoguing doesn't work as well unless we intensely care.

The dialogue process also helps us carry within ourselves the aspects of relationship we tend to seek in the other. In this way you both expand your understanding of the relationship as well as give more. The result can be a peace that comes from greater acceptance and wholeness. For an in-depth explanation of the many possibilities of the inner dialogue method, I urge the reader to read Ira Progoff's *At a Journal Workshop*, as well as his other books.

A word about Progoffs Intensive Journal method. It has been useful to me for over twenty years, and I have taught it for more than fifteen. I and many others owe it a great debt, for it provides a way to work with depth potentials as you work through transitions. Key to its philosophy is the observation that individuals move through cycles of creativity. Growth does not take place in a straight line but moves by delays and diverse directions. Within us are seeds of potential, dependent on the right conditions and time for development.

Just as nature has seasons, so does our growth. My favorite analogy is the tulip bulb. If we cut it open to see what's inside, we kill it. It has to be placed underground and allowed to grow in its own time. Essential is the very cold stage where nothing is visible on the surface. This corresponds to those phases of our lives when we feel as if nothing is happening. Everything seems cold, dark, and lonely. Then in spring the first delicate shoots are put forth, just as in our creativity the fresh ideas emerge. It is important at this stage to be careful because these tender shoots are easily crushed. The stem (or idea, plan, relationship) gets bigger and stronger. A bud, then a blossom is formed. The flowering is the stage we all love and crave. But some plants may bloom only once or twice a lifetime, while some may bloom many times.

Then comes an equally crucial stage in any work or relationship. That is the withering of the bloom, the dying off of what is visible, so that new seeds can be regenerated. When you get attuned to such cycles in your life, you appreciate rhythm and timing more. You can also make transitions from one stage to the next with some understanding of your anxiety and confusion. You cultivate a feeling of oneness with the river of your life, rather than trying to stop this flow and dissect it. You live fully in the world while also creating space for inner, more reflective work. You seek wisdom from your interior rather than depending on others for conventional advice.

Inner dialoguing is a primary tool. You can use it in dialoguing with parental figures or anyone with whom you have been involved, such as I have described in part three, "The Many Lovers."

Dialogue with the Individual

We can dialogue with a person whenever there is a problem or if we just want to open out some issues that we feel need attention. Any person who has strongly attracted us as an Inner Lover would qualify. The dialogue takes place at a deeper level than a face-to-face conversation is likely to. The persons with whom we dialogue may be current lovers, those from the past, and even deceased ones.

Steps in dialoguing:

Let yourself become quiet, close your eyes, and see yourself with this person in your mind.

Write a paragraph about what you feel about this person at the present time in a nonjudgmental, nonanalytical way.

Since the aim is to feel the essence and energy of the other, you should list about ten steps in their life from their point of view, beginning with "I was born" and so on. Sense as much as possible how their life has developed and where it is heading. Doing this procedure can help you put yourself in their shoes and lead to a dialogue that is grounded in reality.

Imagine yourself with the person in a particular setting. Feel the way your disparate lives have moved.

Then, taking your time, let a dialogue take place between the two of you—on paper. Write down what you say and the response of your Inner Lover. Continue until you come to a natural pause but do not quit too soon, as sometimes after a few minutes a dialogue will resume.

You may have quite a lot to say before letting your Inner Lover answer. Or you may joke around in light, short remarks. Let the dialogue flow in whatever way it wants to go, with as little control as possible. The quieter and deeper you are within yourself, the more freely it can develop.

On different occasions your Inner Lover may speak at length to you or reveal just a little. Keep up the dialogues over time as long as certain figures keep appearing in your thoughts or dreams. Dialoguing is a way to get their messages so we can infuse them in our lives.

Here is an extract from a woman's dialogue with a man:

WOMAN: Oh how I ache. I am angry and confused about all this clamoring for sex. All I have is the memory of his embrace. How can I connect with him so the pain goes away? He related to me once with admiration. There was warmth in his eyes. Why can't we be closer? Why do I keep dreaming of him, loving his body?

MAN: To keep you connected here.

WOMAN: But why?

MAN: Because it isn't over yet. Remember, I am a modern man in modern pain, seeking my own answers.

WOMAN: Without a woman.

MAN: Without demands. I want to be free, comfortable. Maybe someday you'll choose not to be in a relationship.

WOMAN: I can't imagine it. I need it.

MAN: You can direct yourself to a creative task, going down, yielding to your love. In that way I can guide you.

WOMAN: But it is in my body that the fires are clamoring for release.

MAN: Heat, intensity, change. . . . Unfulfilled sex becomes smoke or spirit. The flame burns. It becomes smoke—transparent, transformed in the process of consuming you. You need to burn.

WOMAN: For what?

MAN: Color, richness.

WOMAN: But how can I fulfill my hungers?

MAN: By letting this orgasm fill all your holes. Be like a sponge, absorbing all my sperm everywhere in your mouth, eyes, nose, ears, vessel, navel, arms, thighs, fingers, toes. Take it all in.

WOMAN: But why do I think of meeting you on the street and embracing you with joy?

MAN: Because of the difference between what you want and what happens. The way you interiorize me, though, is living the relationship and has an effect. . . . Make an art work. Make yourself me in a story. Be a man instead of living through one. On paper it could be freeing. Don't bind yourself or cling to me.

WOMAN: Why does sex connect me to the cosmos? I feel you as divine but your real self disappears.

MAN: Because the energy is in you. It is your consciousness. Let it show, fill, and satisfy you.

This woman went on to write a screenplay, using the man as her main character.

Dialogue with the Relationship

Dialoguing with the relationship itself is another way to check out what belongs to the personal bond and what is of larger import to yourself As described earlier, every relationship has a life of its own. When you want to find out where the relationship is going and what meaning it has for you, you can dialogue with the relationship itself. Important relationships can seem very bewildering at times, for example whenever feelings snarl or dramatic events, such as an illness or job loss, occur. It's possible to dialogue with the significance of the relationship to your life as a whole.

The procedure is similar to the previous dialogue. Write a short descriptive statement about where the relationship stands at the present time. Then list about ten steps in the history of the relationship from its inception to the present, from the relationship's point of view, as if it were a living being, a third player. For

example, the relationship might have begun when a friend introduced you. You would write: "(1) It began when X introduced
us." And so on. After you sit with your feelings for a while, let a
dialogue spontaneously take place between you and it.

Here is an excerpt from a dialogue by a man who had just met
a woman he was interested in; it cut through his worry by giving
him a sense of how the relationship would grow:

MAN: What is the meaning of this relationship?

RELATIONSHIP: Deb is forlorn, yet independent; intriguing appearance, NYC club scene that you wanted. You are soft, mushy,
and passive. She is all direct push. Also elusive and enticing.
She's everything you are not. That's why you want her so badly.

M: Is there anything that can be good?

R: You'll complement each other.

M: What do I mean to her?

R: Loyalty and support. You have a great capacity for the kind
of companionship that neither of you has ever had. It's an
extraordinary closeness and you have a chance to live it. You
can become very close.

M: And love each other?

R: And love each other.

Dialogue with an Inner Wisdom Figure

The foregoing dialogues have been concerned with actual persons and your relationship with them. To dialogue with figures
you don't know—animals, mythical beings, goddesses, God, or
Buddha—is to move into the transpersonal realm. With them we
explore the meaning in our experiences as our philosophies of
life evolve. Examples of this are the inner wisdom dialogues with
mythical beings, the horse-man Tishnar and the goddess Aphrodite, that are described in the chapter "Reverberations of a Brief
Encounter."

With this type of dialogue you need not make any descriptive statement or steps in the relationship. You simply visualize
yourself in the presence of your chosen subject when you feel
like opening your heart to get access to their wisdom. Exploring

your connection with muses or stars would fall into this domain. Addressing admired figures, such as authors, political leaders, wise grandfathers, and so on, about their lives and work can help you understand yours more.

Here is an example of a dialogue with artist Georgia O'Keeffe.

X: I'd be scared of you if I were in the same room with you.

G: Why?

X: You look so determined, hard, unshakable.

G: I had to be determined. If I was nice, the other person would get what I wanted. You were taught to wait and defer, not to ask or take what you wanted.

X: I want to be committed as an artist but I am afraid of the misery it caused you. It seemed to rule you and make you unhappy.

G: It made me very happy too. Like those gorgeous flowers and shells and skies I painted. My excursions into hills, watching moons, sunsets, dawns.

X: But you didn't paint those. Why not?

G: I tried for the effect of them. I left the realism to Ansel Adams.

X: But why distort? Why didn't you want to duplicate the beauty you saw?

G: Because it wasn't enough. I had to trust my inner being to show me what to do and then I would execute it. Often it didn't work.

X: You believed in your images. You trusted them?

G: A lot more than my teachers.

X: Stieglitz made it easy for you to commit yourself to art. You could quit your job and be nurtured by him. I am afraid to choose that road for myself because I don't see a Stieglitz, nor would I want to be bound to one. I've had no teachers.

G: You are lucky.

X: But I'm not sure what I do is beautiful.

G: You rush and suffer from lack of slow consideration and germination. Things have life but it has to flower within you. You have to give it the space. I protected that and got energy from it. That seemed very powerful.

X: You seem very earthy and body oriented.

G: Creating in the head is sterile and dry.

X: You also did not let people impose on you.

G: You *have* let everyone—mother, father, husband, children—impose on you.

X: You didn't mind being selfish, thinking only of your work.

G: Nah, you create out of guilt and loneliness. Descend into your own creativity.

As a result of this dialogue, the woman felt more committed to finding her own images, to go after what she liked despite others' opinions, and to take more time letting images take shape inside her.

Weaving dreams and images into the fabric of your life in the ways suggested above will help you bring to the fore the potentials unfolding in your psyche. The heat of your love fuels the process. You take your messages from the interior and use them in the art of living and creating. As you are enlarged, so also is the world.

Checklist

As a parting reminder on ways to use the Inner Lover in working on life's problems, here is a checklist:

- Keep track of your dreams with beloved figures and amplify them.
- Record fantasies and imagery experiences.
- Practice the dialogue method.
- Diligently distinguish between the separate realities of the Inner Lover and the outer person.
- Don't block any feelings.
- Have faith that creative transformation will occur.
- Trust in the timing of the psyche.
- Keep in mind the three wills of desire: yours, the other's, and the third player's (the relationship itself).
- Remember that suffering must be long to work its changes and therefore be compassionate toward yourself and others.
- Surrender wholeheartedly to the intimacy of love and you will be blessed.

Remember that you are love's song to sing. You find that song by listening and watching within, letting it rise from your desires and visions. Love is not entirely about the other person, but mostly about you and your song. When you can't sleep because you are too excited or too blue, and you feel you just have to do *something*, create out of that joy and heat. Don't give up on love. It has a rhythm and a melody for you to learn and follow to the end.

Notes

In the notes, CW refers to *The Collected Works of C. G. Jung*, 20 vols. (Princeton, N.J.: Princeton University Press, 1967–1978).

The Roots of Desire

1. Robert Bly, *A Little Book on the Human Shadow* (New York: Harper & Row, 1988), p. 29.
2. Thomas P. and Patrick T. Malone, *The Art of Intimacy* (New York: Prentice Hall, 1987), p. 246.
3. Robert Hass, "Privilege of Being," in *Human Wishes* (New York: Ecco Press, 1989).
4. James Hillman, *Inter Views* (New York: Harper & Row, 1983), p. 178.
5. Anne Carson, *EROS the Bittersweet* (Princeton, N.J.: Princeton University Press, 1986), p. 62.
6. Ethel S. Person, *Dreams of Love and Fateful Encounters* (New York: W. W. Norton, 1988), p. 133.
7. Ibid., p. 93.

Parents in Adulthood

1. Ann Ulanov, *Receiving Woman* (Philadelphia: Westminster Press, 1981), p. 68.

Love Buds

1. Lawrence Kutner, "What Emotions Lie Behind Puppy Love?" *New York Times*, 16 February 1989.

Stars

1. William Grimes, "Demigods Aren't Forever," *New York Times*, 10 November 1991.

Psyche and Eros

1. Erich Neumann, *Amor and Psyche: The Psychic Development of the Feminine* (Princeton, N.J.: Princeton University Press, 1956), p. 136.
2. James Hillman, *The Myth of Analysis* (New York: Harper & Row, 1972), p. 92.

Long-Lasting Bonds

1. Anne Truitt, *Turn* (New York: Viking Press, 1986), p. 33.
2. Ibid.
3. Garrison Keillor, "The Heart of the Matter," *New York Times*, 14 February 1989.

Love's Eternal Triangle

1. John R. Haule, *Divine Madness: Archetypes of Romantic Love* (Boston: Shambhala Publications, 1990), p. 207.
2. Ibid., p. 235.
3. Anne Carson, *EROS the Bittersweet*, p. 168.

4. Ibid., p. 155.
5. Ibid., p. 166.

The Inner Lover in Therapy

1. C G. Jung. *The Symbolic Life* (CW 18), p. 144.
2. Ethel S. Person, *Dreams of Love and Fateful Encounters*, p. 254.
3. H. G. Whittington, "Therapy's Tender Trap," *Savvy*, June 1981, pp. 51–53.

Impossible or Inappropriate Lovers

1. Jung, *Visions Seminars I* (Zurich: Spring Publications, 1976), p. 110.
2. Lucy Ferriss, "Love and Learn" *New York Times*, 29 September 1991.

Eros and Timing

1. Nikos Kazantzakis, *Zorba the Greek* (Oxford: Bruno Cassirer, 1959), pp. 129–130.

Inner Marriage

1. Erich Neumann, *Art and the Creative Unconscious* (New York, Pantheon, 1959), pp. 140–141.
2. Ibid.

Rage, Grief, and Surrender

1. Jean Houston, *The Search for the Beloved* (Los Angeles: Jeremy P. Tarcher, 1985), p. 104.
2. Ibid., p. 117.
3. James Hillman, *Blue Fire* (New York: Harper & Row, 1989), p. 283.

The Creative Offspring

1. Anaïs Nin, *The Diary of Anaïs Nin*, vol. 1 (New York: Swallow Press and Harcourt, Brace & World, 1966), p. 107.
2. Anaïs Nin, *The Diary of Anaïs Nin*, vol. 2 (New York: Swallow Press and Harcourt, Brace & World, 1967), p. 233.
3. Marion Woodman, *The Pregnant Virgin* (Toronto: Inner City Books, 1985), p. 155.
4. Jung, *Psychological Types* (CW 6), p. 193.
5. Denis Donoghue, "The Temptation of St. Tom," *New York Times*, 16 October 1988.
6. Sukie Colegrave, *By Way of Pain* (Rochester, Vt.: Park Street Press, 1988), p. 13.

Spirit Blossoms

1. Margo Anand, *The Art of Sexual Ecstasy* (Los Angeles: Jeremy P. Tarcher, 1989), p. 49.
2. Jean Houston, *The Search for the Beloved*, p. 125.
3. Coleman Barks and John Moyne, *This Longing: Versions of Rumi* (Putney, Vt.: Threshold Books, 1988), p. 64.

A Gift to Oneself and the World

1. Jean Houston, *The Search for the Beloved*, p. 127.
2. Brian Swimme, *The Universe Is a Green Dragon* (Santa Fe, N.M.: Bear & Co., 1985), p. 48.
3. Danah Zohar, *The Quantum Self* (New York: William Morrow, 1990), p. 236.
4. Larry Dossey, *Space, Time, and Medicine* (Boston: Shambhala Publications, 1982), p. 209.
5. E. O. Wilson, *On Human Nature* (Cambridge: Harvard University Press, 1978), p. 4.
6. Jonathan Lear, *Love and Its Place in Nature* (New York: Farrar, Straus, and Giroux, 1990), p. 177.
7. Ibid., p. 217.

8. Ira Progoff, *The Practice of Process Meditation* (New York: Dialogue House Library, 1982), p. 20.
9. Ibid., p. 41.
10. Ibid., p. 53.
11. Ibid., p. 54.

Working with Dreams and Images

1. Jean Houston, *The Search for the Beloved*, p. 131.
2. June Singer, "Sexual Meditation," *New Realities*, May-June 1987.
3. Ira Progoff, *At a Journal Workshop* (New York: Dialogue House Library, 1975), p. 229.
4. Jung, *The Symbolic Life* (cw 18), p. 223.
5. Ibid., p. 258.
6. Sharon Whitehill, "Voices from the Night," *A Women's Diaries Miscellany* (Weston, Conn.: Magic Circle Press, 1989), p. 170.
7. Robert Johnson, *Inner Work* (New York: Harper & Row, 1986), p. 140.
8. Jeremy Taylor, *Dream Work* (New York: Paulist Press, 1983), pp. 150–151.
9. Jung, *Memories, Dreams, Reflections* (New York: Random House, 1965), p. 192.

Bibliography

Anand, Margo. *The Art of Sexual Ecstasy*. Los Angeles: Jeremy P. Tarcher, 1989.

Bachelard, Gaston. *On Poetic Imagination and Reverie*. Dallas: Spring Publications, 1987.

Barks, Coleman, and John Moyne. *This Longing: Versions of Rumi*. Putney, Vt.: Threshold Books, 1988.

Bly, Robert. *A Little Book on the Human Shadow*. New York: Harper & Row, 1988.

Carson, Anne. *Eros the Bittersweet*. Princeton, N.J.: Princeton University Press, 1986.

Colegrave, Sukie. *By Way of Pain*. Rochester, Vt.: Park Street Press, 1988.

Dossey, Larry. *Space, Time, and Medicine*. Boston: Shambhala Publications (New Science Library), 1982.

Hall, Nor. *The Moon and the Virgin: Reflections on the Archetypal Feminine*. New York: Harper & Row, 1980.

Haule, John R. *Divine Madness: Archetypes of Romantic Love*. Boston: Shambhala Publications, 1990. Published in paperback as *Pilgrimage of the Heart: The Path of Romantic Love*. Boston: Shambhala Publications, 1992.

Henderson, Julie. *The Lover Within*. New York: Station Hill Press, 1986.

Hillman, James. *Blue Fire*. New York: Harper & Row, 1989.

————. *The Myth of Analysis*. New York: Harper & Row, 1972.

————, with Laura Pozzo. *Inter Views*. New York: Harper & Row, 1983.

Houston, Jean. *The Search for the Beloved*. Los Angeles: Jeremy P. Tarcher, 1985.

Johnson, Robert. *Inner Work*. New York: Harper & Row, 1986.

Jung, C. G. *The Collected Works of C. G. Jung*. 20 vols. Princeton, N.J.: Princeton University Press, 1967–1978.

————. *Memories, Dreams, Refections*. Edited by Aniela Jaffé. New York: Random House, 1965.

Jung, Emma. *Animus and Anima*. Dallas: Spring Publications, 1957.

Lear, Jonathan. *Love and Its Place in Nature*. New York: Farrar, Straus, and Giroux, 1990.

Malone, Thomas P, and P. T. Malone. *The Art of Intimacy*. New York: Prentice Hall, 1987.

May, Rollo. *Love and Will*. New York: W. W. Norton, 1969.

Neumann, Erich. *Amor and Psyche: The Psychic Development of the Feminine*. Princeton, N.J.: Princeton University Press, 1956.

————. *Art and the Creative Unconscious*. New York: Pantheon Books, 1959.

Nin, Anaïs. *The Diary of Anais Nin*, vols. 1 and 2. New York: Swallow Press and Harcourt, Brace & World, 1966, 1967.

Person, Ethel. *Dreams of Love and Fateful Encounters*. New York: W W. Norton, 1988.

Progoff, Ira. *At a Journal Workshop*. New York: Dialogue House Library, 1975.

————. *The Practice of Process Meditation*. New York: Dialogue House Library, 1982.

Qualls-Corbett, Nancy. *The Sacred Prostitute, Eternal Aspect of the Feminine*. Toronto: Inner City Books, 1988.

Singer, Jerome L. *The Inner World of Daydreaming*. New York: Harper & Row, 1975.

Storr, Anthony. *Solitude, A Return to the Self*. New York: Macmillan, 1988.

Swimme, Brian. *The Universe Is a Green Dragon.* Sante Fe, N.M.: Bear & Co., 1985.

Taylor, Jeremy. *Dream Work.* New York: Paulist Press, 1983.

Truitt, Anne. *Daybook.* New York: Penguin, 1984.

————. *Turn.* New York: Viking Press, 1986.

Welwood, John (ed.). *Challenge of the Heart: Love, Sex, and Intimacy in Changing Times.* Boston: Shambhala Publications, 1985.

Wheelwright, Jane. *Women and Men.* San Francisco: C. G. Jung Institute, 1978.

Wilson, E. O. *On Human Nature.* Cambridge: Harvard University Press, 1978.

Woodman, Marion. *The Pregnant Virgin.* Toronto: Inner City Books, 1985.

Zohar, Danah. *The Quantum Self.* New York: William Morrow, 1990.